Transportation Systems Evaluation

Transportation Systems Evaluation

Peter R. Stopher
Northwestern University

Arnim H. Meyburg
Cornell University

Lexington Books
D.C. Heath and Company
Lexington, Massachusetts
Toronto

Library of Congress Cataloging in Publication Data

Stopher, Peter R
   Transportation systems evaluation.
   Includes bibliographical references and index.
   1. Local transit—Mathematical models. 2. Transportation plan-
ning. 3. System analysis. I. Meyburg, Arnim H., joint author. II. Ti-
tle.
HE305.S839   388.4   74-25057
ISBN 0-699-96958-3

Published simultaneously in Canada

Printed in the United States of America

International Standard Book Number: 0-669-96958-3

Library of Congress Catalog Card Number: 74-25057

To our parents,

Joan and Harold Stopher
and
Auguste and Friedel
Meyburg

Contents

viii

List of Figures

List of Tables

Preface

Like our earlier book, *Urban Transportation Modeling and Planning,* this book has evolved from course notes developed by the authors over the last several years at Cornell University, McMaster University, and Northwestern University. Over these years, we have found there to be no single text that encompasses both sides of transportation-systems evaluation—economic evaluation and the analysis of impacts or consequences.

Our courses have been offered to senior-level undergraduates and first-year and second-year graduate students in transportation and planning programs. The book also is aimed at these groups for academic purposes. We believe, however, that the book will also be useful to practicing professionals who wish to learn about evaluation procedures, or who need a reference suitable for augmenting their existing capabilities in this area. This book is also intended to complement *Urban Transportation Modeling and Planning,* which gave evaluation a rather cursory treatment within the context of the transportation-planning process and the associated modeling techniques.

We have assumed that the reader of this book will possess a rudimentary knowledge of basic microeconomics and will be acquainted with the concepts of supply, demand, consumer surplus, and general consumer behavior. In addition, we assume some familiarity with the urban transportation-planning process and particularly with the process of decision making among alternative transportation strategies. Beyond this, we have attempted to present to the reader all that he or she will need to know within the pages of this book, although some knowledge of the systems-analytic framework, as applied to transportation, will also be found to be helpful.

As we have already indicated, the principal purpose of this book is to present a detailed treatment of the alternative evaluation techniques for transportation-system strategies. While we have discussed the techniques in the context of transportation, the evaluation procedures are equally relevant for many other public-sector decisions, such as in water resources, education, and fire protection. The book focuses on two principal procedures—economic evaluation and cost-effectiveness evaluation.

The first three chapters address a number of fundamentals of the economic-evaluation procedure and comprise the background against which the procedure is developed. These fundamentals include a discussion of the basic answers required from any evaluation process, together with a description of both past and current practice in modifying these answers to the transportation situation for economic evaluation. Chapter 4 examines the theory and practice of placing monetary values on the savings of travel time that are frequently a major element of the benefits of transportation investments. Much controversy surrounds the methods of valuing travel time, as well as the relevance of doing so at all. We have attempted to summarize many of these arguments and to offer the reader sufficient information to form his own opinion.

In chapter 5, the economic-evaluation methods are presented and their use is demonstrated through an example. This establishes a base point for the comparison of alternative methods. In addition, the shortcomings of an economic evaluation become clear.

The next two chapters—6 and 7—are concerned with a broader examination of the consequences of transportation investments. Chapter 6 reviews the consequences that affect both users and nonusers and outlines the existing level of knowledge about the measurement and prediction of these consequences. Chapter 7 describes and illustrates a framework within which these consequences may be taken into account in making decisions between alternative strategies. Finally, chapter 8 reviews both types of evaluation techniques discussed in the earlier chapters, compares the techniques, and outlines our perceptions of the directions for future research.

It has been our experience that the material covered by this book is sufficient to occupy a three-semester-hour or four-quarter-hour course. Clearly, there are many issues basic to any evaluation procedure in the public sector to which we have given only cursory attention in the interests of maintaining an adequate one-course treatment of the topic. We have attempted to lead the reader to other sources for these issues through the notes for each chapter. We recommend that the serious student use these reference materials in as comprehensive a manner as possible to gain a thorough understanding of the subject matter.

We feel it is also important to point out that we have endeavored to make our own positions clear on all controversial issues discussed in this book. Nevertheless, we do not believe that the last word has been said on any of these issues and we would encourage the reader to study all viewpoints before forming his own position. Again, the various references listed in the notes will be found helpful in doing this.

Acknowledgments

Many individuals and agencies have contributed to the development and preparation of this book. We would like to express our sincere thanks to all of them. In particular, we would like to acknowledge the considerable efforts of Valerie Stopher and Patricia Apgar, who typed the manuscript and bore with us patiently as we made numerous changes to it. We were, again, most fortunate to have the use of the drafting skills of Wilfred R. Sawbridge of Cornell University, who prepared all of the drawings for this book. We would like to thank John Coulter of Cornell University, who worked extensively on the computer program for the examples of chapter 5. His efforts and dedication were instrumental in the writing of that chapter. We would also like to thank Dian Younker of Northwestern University, who read the entire manuscript and offered many useful critical comments on both the style and content of the book.

Many students have contributed to this book through their responses to course notes that formed the original document for this book. In addition, we have learned much from their questions in class, their term papers, and their evaluations of the courses that underlie this book.

The authors would also like to acknowledge the cooperation of Rotterdam University Press for permission to quote from *The Determinants of Travel Mode Choice in Dutch Cities* by F.X. de Donnea; the Transportation Research Board, National Academy of Sciences, for permission to quote and use illustrations from *NCHRP Reports Numbers 96 and 156*; the New York Academy of Sciences for permission to quote from *Transportation: A Service* by John de S. Coutinho (editor); the McGraw-Hill Book Company for permission to quote from *Systems Analysis for Engineers and Planners* by M. Wohl and B.V. Martin; and D.C. Heath and Company for permission to use an illustration from *Urban Transportation Modeling and Planning* by P.R. Stopher and A.H. Meyburg.

The authors accept complete responsibility for any errors that might still exist in the text.

**Transportation Systems
Evaluation**

1

Purpose and Basic Concepts of Evaluation

General Definitions

All rational decision making, whether by individuals or groups of individuals, involves some form of evaluation. This evaluation can take an almost unlimited range of forms and levels of sophistication, depending upon the decision involved, the decision maker, and characteristics of the courses of action contemplated. The context of concern in this book is the selection of a policy or the decision to invest public funds in transportation projects. In order to understand the meaning of evaluation and the development of procedures for evaluation in the public sector, a few illustrations and some background are appropriate.

Evaluation may be termed the relative and absolute assessment of the worthwhileness of a particular course of action or planned expenditure. Worthwhileness can be assessed in a number of ways. For example, there is a question of to whom any plan is worthwhile, and the question of when it will be worthwhile. In addition there is a basic question of determining the units of worthwhileness. Some of the problems raised by these questions are revealed in the following examples.

In terms of the individual, each of us is continually making decisions by weighing the alternatives and deciding whether to use available limited resources in one way or another, or whether to retain those resources for the present and do nothing. For instance, one may have $1,000 saved and be contemplating buying a new car. Given certain preconceived biases, an individual would compare perhaps two or three specific models. These comparisons will include prices, performance, and other characteristics of each model. The individual may also have an existing car, which is now getting somewhat old and is beginning to run up increasingly large repair bills, as well as consuming greater and greater quantities of gasoline and oil per mile. In this example, a loan will also be a necessary part of the purchase. In comparing models, one evaluates the "worth" of each of the various characteristics, e.g., How much is a top speed of 110 mph worth? How much are bucket seats worth?

Assuming that the individual is conscientious in his evaluation, he may next compute the annual costs of each alternative, comprising running costs, maintenance, repairs and replacement parts, depreciation, and the annual interest on a loan to finance the new car. In assessing the possibil-

1

ity of retaining the old car, the interest that the $1,000 will earn if invested should be deducted. As a result of all this, a decision can be made between alternatives on the basis of their respective worth. Clearly, in such a case, the question To whom is it worthwhile? is simply answered—to the individual.

Some dilemmas can be explored from this example. For instance, should the individual be concerned with the size of the car because of the quantity of scarce resources consumed in the construction of the car, e.g., aluminum, petroleum derivatives, steel, and rubber? Should he also be concerned with the efficiency of the engine from either or both of the viewpoints of gasoline consumption and production of emissions? These concerns represent elements of a broader viewpoint than that of the single individual. Thus, it raises the question of viewpoint for the evaluation. It also raises the question of measurement of worthwhileness, since these elements are not readily reflected in cost terms in the present market. A final question raised by this example is that of the extent of an individual's social accountability.

The illustration may be continued by considering the activities of private sector firms and corporations. An initial level of evaluation is conducted by the relevant experts of the firm. The products of this evaluation—a short list of alternative projects, investments, or other courses of action—are then subjected to a further evaluation by a board, or other similarly-constituted body of "laymen." In certain instances, the decision may be subjected to a vote of the shareholders. In general, these evaluations may be characterized as being based upon a single criterion—the profit, or relative profit, to be obtained. That this evaluation procedure is insufficient is clearly demonstrated by the recent promulgation of legislation that is aimed at making private industry decisions more responsive to public values as interpreted by government. Therefore, it can again be seen that the traditional private industry evaluation usually considers worthwhileness to the firm, unless forced to consider a broader viewpoint by legislation; that it measures worthwhileness in monetary terms (i.e., will the course of action enhance the value of the company and the returns to shareholders?); and that it subjects the evaluation to scrutiny by the board of directors of the firm and sometimes by the shareholders. This scrutiny should ensure that the evaluation process is effective within the constraints of the viewpoint and value system adopted by the firm.

It is apparent, first, that evaluation should be carried out on plans for public investment, i.e., government expenditure. It is also apparent that a direct extension of the private sector evaluation cannot operate in the case of public sector decisions, since there is no way to scrutinize the evaluation mechanism through the equivalent of a board of directors or the shareholders. Furthermore, the government (at any level) is not in the business of profit making in pure monetary terms. In fact, its involvement in many sectors is predicated on the fact that investments in those sectors are, by nature, unprofitable. Worthwhileness of public sector actions cannot, therefore, be measured in a form analogous to those of the private sector. One might propose that worthwhileness be measured in terms of "welfare." However, there are no standard procedures for estimating welfare and measuring it for inclusion in a decision making process. Viewpoint again becomes crucial here. Whose welfare is to be increased? A course of action that increases the welfare of one locality may decrease the welfare of a neighboring locality. For example, a freeway may be routed past village A, relieving congested roads and improving access to other locations in the region. The same freeway may then pass through village B, requiring relocation of houses and businesses, increasing the noise and pollution exposures along the line of the freeway, and cutting off many cross highways. If net welfare is increased, is the freeway justified?

Finally, there is no other agency or administration beyond the Federal government that can ensure social responsiveness of public sector decisions—the role often assumed by government in relation to the private sector. Thus, the evaluation procedures used in the public sector must be able to incorporate a responsiveness to broad social concerns.

These problems of public sector evaluation can be illustrated specifically within the transportation sector. With a few exceptions, mass transport is provided by public authorities, or by private companies that are partially subsidized by city, state, or federal authorities. Highways are, without exception, provided by public authorities. The specific question that arises here is To whom should alternatives be worthwhile when being assessed by a public body? For instance, should a state, in considering a highway project that it may finance, be concerned with the highway user alone? Alternatively, should it be concerned with the people whose money is being spent, i.e., the population of the state? Or should it take an even wider view and consider the benefits to the nation as a whole?[1]

Further complications are added by the fact that any improved or new transportation facility (where "facility" is to be construed as either a physical facility or a policy, regulatory scheme, or other change in transportation supply) will have effects on the remainder of the transportation network. This network will include federal, state, and local facilities. Thus, the building of a federally funded freeway will have effects on the volumes of traffic on adjacent highways, which may include both state and locally funded highways. The changed volumes on these adjacent facilities may cause more frequent maintenance to be necessary, and may even require widening and upgrading of some of the facilities to cope safely with the increased volumes. Should the federal government, in this case, consider the economics of the project only in terms of its own expenditures, or should it include the concomitant expenditures by the state and local authorities?

To a large extent, economists and transportation planners cannot agree on a single "correct" approach in this area.[2] Some argue that a national viewpoint should be taken in the evaluation of transportation plans. However, differing views exist on whether the economics should be considered only with respect to the specific agency concerned, or to all the agencies affected by the project.

Another position that is taken, which is of more benefit in considering privately-financed projects, such as toll highways, is to consider the economic feasibility from the viewpoint of those whose funds are being risked, i.e., those who will have to carry the costs if the anticipated benefits do not accrue. Clearly, this alternative will often lead to considerations in terms of the national economy, since federal funds or federal credit backing are usually a major part of the funds used in any transportation project.

It should be noted that traditionally highway and mass transportation plans have been evaluated from the point of view of the user alone. Thus, only the costs and benefits accruing to users have been incorporated in the economic analysis of alternative plans. In addition to describing methods of economic analysis, this book will also identify and discuss nonuser consequences and potential ways of incorporating these into the evaluation.

Measuring Worth

One of the major questions raised in the preceding discussion is that of the measurement of worthwhileness. It has clearly been established that public sector actions cannot be evaluated in terms of the monetary profit that accrues from a specific course of action. The individual car buyer and the private corporation can make their decisions in monetary terms. In terms of replacing the old car, the costs to be incurred include the money cost of the new car, the cost of borrowing money, and the loss of interest being earned by the money used for the down payment. The "profits" would include lower running and maintenance costs of the new car compared with the old one, an increase in financial assets, and the trade-in or net selling price of the old car. All of these items can be measured in simple monetary terms, and represent a balance-sheet assessment of the intended course of action. The inclusion of any other considerations, such as reliability, comfort, and prestige, render the evaluation more complex by extending it beyond its pure monetary base.

Without the consideration of nonmonetary items, the problem is relatively simple. The individual has not taken account of such things as the capacity of highways on which he or she wishes to use his or her vehicle, the impacts of noise, pollution, etc. on other people and the environment. In other words, the alternatives have been assessed from the individual's viewpoint alone. Similarly, the private firm or business is confronted with a relatively simple set of answers, based upon a similar monetary assessment and frequently without the inclusion of intangible or nonmonetary profits or losses.

In considering public sector investments, it is appropriate, as indicated earlier, to change the nomenclature and consider costs of actions and the benefits that might accrue,[3] rather than the profits. The use of the term "benefits" is an attempt to introduce the idea of welfare into the evaluation process. Furthermore, both costs and benefits may be interpreted in very broad terms, not restricted to monetary elements alone. These concepts are consistent with the systems-analysis framework[4] used for transportation planning. This framework is shown in Figure 1-1, from which it can be seen that evaluation is a central element of the process. In idealized terms, the evaluation process requires the input of both the values, goals, objectives, and criteria, and the consequences forecast by the system model for each alternative. The product of the evaluation is either input to the selection process or identification of the fact that there are no acceptable alternatives in the tested set. The terms "costs" and "benefits" are to be interpreted as comprising the measures of the consequences of an alternative, where these are to be assessed against the criteria and objectives.

The systems-analytic framework and the adoption of the terms "costs" and "benefits," however, render no material assistance in defining the appropriate measures of worthwhileness. A number of answers are possible and the "correctness" of any one cannot be determined. In the past, the definitions have been, implicitly or explicitly, the money costs and money benefits of a project as they are applicable to the user. This includes using dollar equivalents for items such as time and accidents as part of the analysis.[5] The dollar equivalents of time and accidents have been based on inferred values only.

More generally, it could be stated that the factors comprising worthwhileness should be all those factors for which the public is willing to pay or trade off other items of value where conflicts arise. Thus, social, political, and environmental factors can be included in the analysis where there is evidence that society is prepared to forgo certain resources and substitute other resources of real value. Lack of willingness to forgo such resources in order to achieve a social, political, or environmental objective is indicative of a lack of real value for that objective, and it therefore has no place in economic analysis. It is a *presumed* rather than a *real* concern.[6]

The inclusion, in the evaluation, of the impacts of a facility or program

6

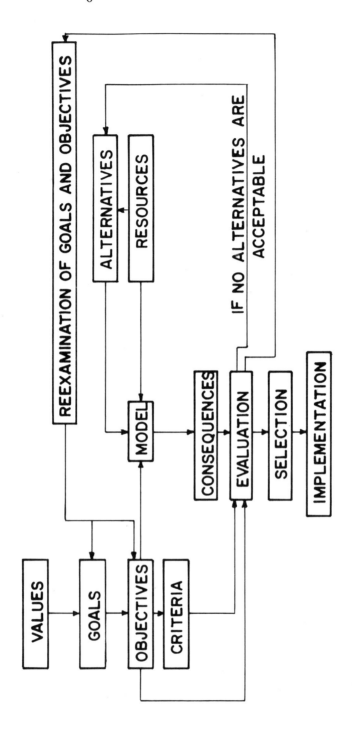

Figure 1-1. Systems Analysis Procedure in Flow Diagram Form.

on urban or rural growth and land use *should* take place in the evaluation process. Nevertheless, as will be seen with this and certain social, environmental, and political consequences, the ability to include such effects in quantitative terms, with a knowledge of the cause-and-effect relationships involved, does not currently exist, particularly in the field of transportation.

A brief statement has already been made indicating that the costs and benefits considered are those of the user. In ideal terms, as is discussed in chapter 6, the evaluation should consider all users and nonusers who are affected by a proposed alternative. As an example of this, the customary position taken in past transportation project evaluation has been to take into account only those costs and benefits that accrue to facility users (again, using facility in its broadest sense) and to ignore all others.[7] At least two obvious reasons exist for this position. First, in early project evaluations, there was a general lack of awareness of the extent of nonuser costs and benefits. The environmental and social effects of highway construction, for example, were largely unrecognized. Second, there is considerable difficulty in determining who the nonusers are. These may include those who live close to or along the line of the proposed facility. It may also include those who travel on parallel or cross-highways, who may encounter either reduced or increased congestion as a result of the proposed facility. The nonuser may also include all of those who are affected by the diminution of resources that occurs with the construction of a facility. Thus, there is considerable difficulty in identifying who the nonusers are. This is discussed further in chapter 6.

In summary, two necessary answers have been given here to questions of worth for public sector investments. First, the measurement of worth has been defined as comprising measurement of the costs and benefits of the alternative projects. The questions of how to measure these or place values upon nonmonetary benefits are addressed later in this book. The second question that has been answered here is that of viewpoint. The viewpoint used is that of the facility user.

Timing

The last question to be raised in this chapter is When will an investment be worthwhile? Many of the plans considered for public sector investments require time in order to be achieved. The construction of a new road, for instance, will take several months at least, and may take one or two years, depending upon the physical parameters of the facility. In addition, the planning process for such a facility—including land acquisition, design, and preliminary engineering works—may take up to five years before construction is commenced. Major plans for an urban area are often put forward with an expected completion date as much as ten or twenty years in the future. Clearly, the timing of projects will have a considerable effect on the evaluation of associated costs and benefits.

A major problem arises from this, which may be termed "planning under uncertainty." No matter how sophisticated forecasting techniques become, it is certain that planning must continue to be conducted in a state of uncertainty. Essentially, this uncertainty will be caused by the fact that the planners do not have complete control over and understanding of all the factors that make up the environment within which planning takes place. The implications of this for the evaluation process are principally those of the uncertainty of costs and total benefits attributable to a plan by completion.

Nevertheless, given that transportation projects are not constructed instantaneously and that the investments have a protracted lifespan, any evaluation scheme must, to be correct, attempt to account for the costs and benefits of the life of the investment. Thus, evaluation is not to be considered as being conducted at a single instant in time, but rather as concerning the project life. This raises two questions, both of which are dealt with in chapter 3. The first is that of what project life is and the second is how to take account of costs and benefits that accrue over a substantial period of time.

Summary

The evaluation process for transportation plans, and indeed for most public sector projects, is a process for judging the worth of alternative investments, policies, or courses of action in a manner responsive to public needs and welfare. Unlike private-sector evaluations, monetary profit is not the goal of investment by the public sector (although, of course, it can be a desirable outcome) and there is no mechanism for policing the evaluation procedure by outside agencies. Thus, the evaluation procedure must be self-policing and designed to reflect societal values and goals.

Three critical issues arise in designing such an evaluation procedure. The first issue is that of the measurement of worthwhileness. It has been stated here that the traditional approach to transportation evaluation utilizes the concepts of costs and benefits. These are applied only to those factors to which the public is willing to attach values. The second issue is that of the appropriate viewpoint from which to assess worthwhileness. Traditional treatment of viewpoint is to use that of the user of the facility under consideration, although arguments have been put forward for broadening this to include certain impacted nonusers (see chapter 6). Finally, the issue of timing has been identified as a crucial one in the evaluation process. The timing issue introduces the complexity of uncertainty into the analysis, and also dictates the necessity of evaluating projects over their expected life, rather than at a single point in time.

The various issues raised in this chapter are dealt with in detail in the remainder of the book. The initial concerns presented here deal with the traditional transportation-evaluation scheme developed in the context of highway investments, while the latter part of the book is concerned with a broader interpretation of the requirements of evaluation and with the directions of current efforts.

2

Costs, Prices, Benefits, and Consumer Surplus

Costs and Benefits

General

It is clear from the preceding chapter that the definition of the costs and benefits of any particular project are strongly dependent upon the definitions of viewpoint, parameters of worth or value, and the time span of the project. Hence, it is not reasonable to define sets of costs and benefits for all points of view, etc. In this section, those costs and benefits that will be discussed are those that have been included in most past evaluations and those that would be included by taking a broad public viewpoint.

As previously stated, traditional evaluation processes have used the viewpoint of the user alone as the appropriate one for considering costs and benefits. Also, traditionally, only those costs and benefits that can be readily reduced to dollars have been included. Before enumerating the constituent costs and benefits, one further matter must be dealt with. This concerns the dangers of double counting costs. In a situation where tolls or other charges are levied on the user to recoup part or all of the costs of a new facility, these tolls must not be included in the costs in addition to the construction costs. They may only enter at all if they recoup total costs, and are therefore a proxy for construction costs. In that case, either construction costs or tolls, but not both, may be used.

Costs

Five potential categories of costs may be considered in the traditional user-oriented evaluation of highway investments.[1]

1. Construction and land acquisition costs
2. Statutory relocation costs of residences and businesses
3. Maintenance, operation, and administration costs of the new facility
4. User travel costs (principally time and vehicle costs)
5. Accident costs

If a wider approach to evaluation is taken, then some additional items should be added to the above costs. Considered from a broad public view-point, costs should also include:

6. Social costs and nonstatutory, but desirable, relocation
7. Terminal costs

The composition of each of these costs is examined in turn.

The costs of construction and land acquisition comprise the costs of the land, materials, and labor. The conversion of labor resources and construction materials into money costs is not very simple, since changes in costs over time, as they will effect the actual construction program, need to be estimated. Also, the actual costs of labor are not necessarily the true opportunity costs of labor resources. The market price of labor at any time may either understate or overstate the true opportunity cost of those resources. The opportunity cost is the appropriate one to use in the calculation of these elements of project cost.

Relocation costs will comprise the costs of providing new homes and business premises of comparable value to those taken by the facility construction, depending upon federal or state laws. Various states throughout the United States also provide additional compensation such as moving costs and other dislocation benefits.[2]

Operation, maintenance, and administration costs cover the annual costs of operating the facility. These will include such items as maintenance, signing, pavement markings, road surface repair, spraying and cutting of abutting slopes and banks, and snow clearance. They include the annual costs of additional plant capacity to maintain the facility efficiently over and above the costs required for the remainder of the network. In the case of a toll facility, they also include the operation of toll-collecting machinery and the costs of manpower required for this. Administrative costs are somewhat more difficult to estimate, particularly in the case of nontoll facilities. The increase of administrative costs may be difficult to assess in such cases, particularly on relatively small projects, where increases will not appear in increased staff requirements, but only in marginal increases in work load on the existing staff. These costs include the staff needed by the maintaining agency (e.g., state department of transportation) in order to handle the various engineering and other routine or periodic tasks associated with the facility. Administrative costs also include policing costs.

User costs are somewhat more complex and include several items. The first item is vehicle-ownership costs, excluding any fees or taxes that are imposed to recover facility costs. (In the general situation in which public highways are funded by city, state, and federal sources, with funds being derived from general accounts, no taxes or fees should be included in vehicle ownership costs.) The second item is the direct and indirect operating costs, including mileage-related maintenance, but again excluding taxes and fees that help to cover facility costs. Care must be taken to avoid double counting between this item and the previous one. If the replacement parts needed to keep a vehicle in good operating condition are included in ownership costs, then they must be omitted from operating costs. Some disagreement exists in the use of both of the above sets of costs. It may be argued, from a strict economic viewpoint, that only marginal operating costs of the vehicles should be included as part of highway investment costs. This viewpoint would exclude the first set of costs described here—the vehicle-ownership costs. On the other hand, the construction of any new facility will reduce vehicle operating costs sufficiently to induce some people to purchase a car, or an additional car. For these people, it may be said that the marginal costs of travel include vehicle-ownership costs. The estimation of these costs would be extremely difficult, however, since it would entail an estimate of the vehicle-ownership changes induced by a facility. Average vehicle-ownership costs are therefore used as an approximation for this effect. In conclusion, it can be noted at this point that, rightly or wrongly, vehicle-ownership costs are included in user costs.

The third item is time costs. Many arguments are put forward concerning time-cost calculations. In the view of the "strict" economist, only that travel time that is reflected in the gross national product (GNP) may be included in travel-time accounting.[3] Clearly, this leads to the conclusion that only working time spent in travel should be included. The rate at which this travel time is valued is the total market value of the person concerned, i.e., wage rate plus the employer's overhead. This time is clearly paid for out of the gross national product.

The separation of working time spent in travel from the commuting trip raises a difficult distinction. It may be argued that, in large metropolitan areas, wages and working hours reflect, in part, the necessity for long journeys to work and are, thus, related to the travel time. Exactly how this is incorporated in the gross national product is not clear, nor is it readily apparent how a value may be determined for it.

In the view of many transportation analysts, this strict economic viewpoint is not acceptable. It is argued that many investments in transportation are justified on grounds apart from the gross national product, and that all travel time has a "value" or disutility and should therefore be included in any analysis of the economics of a transportation project. This is consistent with the position put forward in chapter 1 that all costs and benefits should be included for which individuals or society exhibit a willingness to trade. This leads to the requirement of determining values for all types of travel time—time spent on business trips, work trips, personal business trips, and recreational trips. The valuation issue is the subject of chapter 4. For now, it may be noted that all travel time involves disutility and, therefore, monetary values of travel time will be needed for all trip purposes on the facility to be evaluated.

Clearly, two further costs should also be included in terms of the user costs, the disutilities of travel discomfort and travel inconvenience. This presents even greater problems than values of travel time for various purposes, since valuation implies the ability to measure comfort and convenience. A discussion of the possible methods and solutions to this problem is not wholly appropriate here.[4] It should be noted, however, that such costs should be included when valid measures for them have been derived. In the meantime, it is probable that the value of travel time will include a proxy for such items in general, although not for specific alternatives, which vary in terms of elements of comfort and convenience.

Accident costs are the next that need to be dealt with. Property damage accidents can be rated at the average amount of damage resulting from accidents, using figures derived from a comparable facility. Frequently, national figures are used for freeways and similar facilities. For personal injury and death, the problems of money costs become more difficult. In the past, these values have usually been based on the average amounts of insurance paid for each class of injury—slight, serious, and fatal.[5]

The final cost is that of terminal facilities. This comprises the costs of terminals (including parking and garaging) incurred by the user in owning or using a vehicle, unless a terminal facility is part of the construction under consideration. In this latter case, problems of double counting can arise again. If the building of a parking garage or other terminal facility is included in the project being evaluated, then the costs to users must not be included, since this will contribute to defraying the construction, maintenance, and administration costs. Again, however, questions of marginal cost pricing can be raised in relation to this element of costs. In applying this argument, terminal costs, like vehicle-ownership costs, are not allowable in the evaluation process.

Benefits

There are, primarily, two elements of benefits that are included in traditional highway-evaluation procedures. These are user travel benefits and intergovernmental transfers. Some exchange between costs and benefits may be considered, such as a reduction in accidents being considered as a benefit. The consideration of intergovernmental transfers as a benefit depends upon the viewpoint taken concerning the agencies involved. If one views the economics within the government as a whole, then intergovernmental transfers have no place in the benefits.

As with costs, a wider approach to evaluation will require that additional benefits be included. From a broad public viewpoint, the benefits should then also include facility-associated nonuser benefits and other nonuser benefits.

In examining benefits, one must establish what constitutes a benefit and how it is measured. Before doing this, brief consideration is given to what the listed benefits might include. User travel benefits include both perceived and unperceived benefits, which are discussed in detail subsequently. Intergovernmental transfers are added to these to allow correct accounting when a lower government agency takes an "agency-only" view of costs and benefits, thus accounting for benefits to higher agencies and departments.

Principally, facility-associated nonuser benefits include revenues derived from nonusers due to property taxes, etc., which are increased because of the amenity value of the facility. These benefits and other nonuser benefits present problems in evaluation. It is clear that social benefits and disbenefits to those who do not use a facility are important. Disbenefits include pollution of air and water, noise, etc. Benefits might include reduced shipping costs for goods, greater amenity through increased accessibility, etc. Yet other benefits may stem from reduced pollution, or noise in cases where traffic is diverted to a new facility from existing streets and highways. Several problems arise in accounting for these externalities. First, although such externalities also arise in the case of investments and actions of private firms and individuals, they have rarely been taken into account in economic evaluations in these areas. There is, however, increasing pressure on public and private industry. to reduce pollution of air and water and to consider other externalities. Inevitably, this is likely to lead to the inclusion of such externalities in investment decisions. Second, generally there are no marketplace values for these externalities. This clearly presents a major problem in assessing external benefits and disbenefits. Again, however, current trends in private and public industry may give rise to a satisfactory value system for such items. Some of these problems are dealt with in chapter 6 at greater length.

A final comment is in order on the relevance of costs and benefits to an evaluation process. In general, there is a complete balancing of all costs and benefits if a sufficiently broad perspective is taken.[6] A reduction in accidents causes a reduction in the earnings of doctors, hospitals, and all the associated staff. Reductions in congestion may lead to reduced gasoline consumption and hence to reduced receipts for gasoline companies. Similarly, balances exist for virtually any cost or benefit associated with an investment. Thus, there would be no relevance for an evaluation process if a global viewpoint were taken since there is no net cost or net benefit for any investment at this level. The key to an appropriate evaluation process is the identification of *relevant* costs and benefits for the specific decision-making process. The identification put forward in this chapter is intended to fulfill this role.

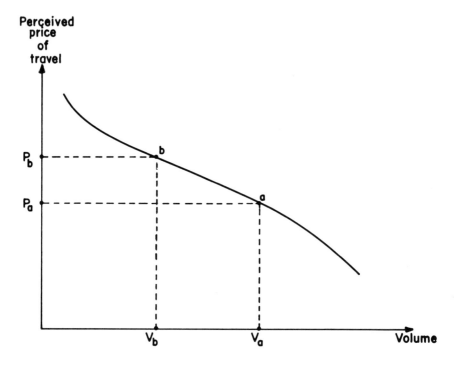

Figure 2-1. Simplified Demand Curve for Travel between i and j.

Perceived Benefit and Consumer Surplus

The previous section defined the constituent elements of benefits in both the traditional highway evaluation process and a more broadly interpreted evaluation process. It is now necessary to consider the measurement of benefit for the evaluation process. In this section, measurement is considered in the context of user benefits alone. However, the approach can be extended without difficulty to the nonuser.

In order to develop the measurement concepts it is necessary to consider the demand and price-volume curves for highway travel.[7] A simplified demand curve is shown in Figure 2-1. This demand curve indicates that, given a perceived travel price of P_a, a volume of V_a people will make a trip between a pair of points, i and j, at the specific time for which P_a is the appropriate price. This curve can clearly be interpreted as giving a measure of the willingness of people to pay for travel. At point b, for instance, where the price is P_b, only a volume of V_b consider the trip to be worthwhile. If the price drops to P_a, a larger volume, V_a, now consider the trip to be worthwhile.

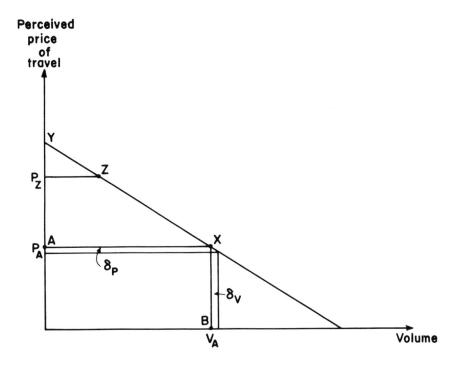

Figure 2-2. Demand Curve Showing δV Travelers at the Margin.

Some concepts necessary in considering the demand curve as a basis for determining benefits must now be defined. First, in the above discussion, if P_b and P_a are each the prices that the travelers actually do pay because of the shape of the demand curve, it is clear that P_b and P_a are only a measure of the willingness of the traveler to pay at the margin. In other words, if the costs were decreased by a small quantity δ_P (see Figure 2-2), the resulting increased volume, δ, represents those travelers to whom the trip is just worth $(P - \delta_P)$. The remaining V travelers would actually be prepared to pay at least P, and many would be prepared to pay quite a lot more. When δ_P is made extremely small, the volume δ_V represents the number of travelers who are at the margin at price $(P - \delta_P)$. This is illustrated in Figure 2-2. The individual who is at X is prepared to pay P_A to travel and will travel if P_A is the perceived price of travel. However, an individual at Z, who is willing to pay P_Z to travel, but is only required to pay P_A, will travel but will realize a "consumer surplus" of $(P_Z - P_A)$. The consumer surplus is, thus, the difference between what an individual is willing to pay and what he perceives he is required to pay, when the former is equal to or exceeds the latter. If perceived price is greater than

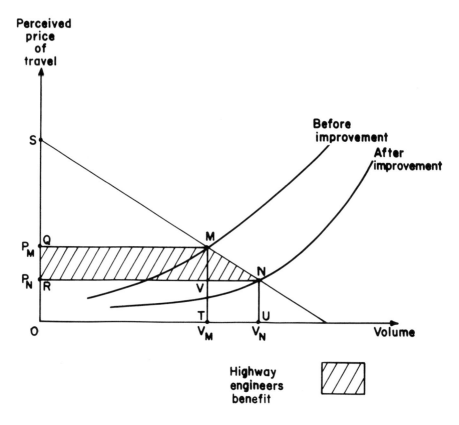

Figure 2-3. Definition of Highway Engineer's Benefit.

willingness to pay, the individual will not purchase the good (travel, in this case). It follows that, if Figure 2-2 represents the demand curve for people desiring to travel between two points, the total consumer surplus accruing to the volume V_A is given by the area AYX. Two important assumptions are implicit in this statement. First, it is assumed that demand curves of different individuals can be aggregated meaningfully into a single demand curve. Second, it is assumed that the entire demand curve can be determined and that it intersects the price axis at a finite perceived price of travel. If the upper end of the demand curve becomes asymptotic to the price axis, or is discontinuous, then total consumer surplus is undefined.

The definition of consumer surplus and the demand curve lead directly to the standard highway engineering definition of benefit. By plotting two price-volume curves and a given demand curve on the same axes as used in Figure 2-2, one may examine the likely result of a potential transportation improvement, as shown in Figure 2-3. Thus, it can be seen that the improvement results in a decrease in price. Two results occur. First, the present travelers, V_M, experience a decrease in their perceived price of travel, resulting in an increase in consumer surplus. Second, new travelers now use the facility, $(V_N - V_M)$, and for most of them there is again some consumer surplus, represented by the triangular area VMN. Given this scenario, objections to the use of consumer surplus on the grounds that it cannot be measured may be dismissed, since only the *change* in consumer surplus is needed. Theoretically, one may object that the use of consumer surplus as the measure of benefit precludes the estimation of benefits from a new facility.[8] However, in a developed country, it is highly improbable that a new facility will represent a change from an infinite to a finite perceived price. Likewise, the definition of users, for the purposes of evaluation, includes the users of an old facility that is to be replaced by a new facility, thus permitting the computation again of a change in consumer surplus resulting from the improvement.

It is worthwhile to consider briefly the alternative to consumer surplus as a measure of benefit, and to consider the arguments for and against each of the potential definitions. The alternative definition[9] excludes consumer surplus and defines the benefit as the change in price for each traveler. Thus, at price P_M in Figure 2-3 the total benefit is the area $SOTM$, while excluding consumer surplus, it is the area $QOTM$. Mathematically, the benefit exclusive of consumer surplus is given by equation (2.1).

$$B_M = V_M P_M \qquad (2.1)$$

Similarly, at price P_N, the benefit, exclusive of consumer surplus, is the area $ROUN$, or equation (2.2).

$$B_N = V_N P_N \qquad (2.2)$$

The change in benefits would, therefore, appear to be given by equation (2.3).

$$\Delta B = V_N P_N - V_M P_M \qquad (2.3)$$

However, this includes the consumer surplus that accrues to the new travelers $(V_N - V_M)$, which, for consistency, must be excluded. Thus, the change in benefits resulting from the improvement is given by the area $VTUN$, or equation (2.4).

$$\Delta B' = P_N (V_N - V_M) \qquad (2.4)$$

This is clearly a markedly different definition of benefit than the former one, thus requiring a careful examination of the arguments for and against each alternative. Two primary arguments can be put forward for excluding consumer surplus and adopting the benefit definition of equation (2.4). First, consumer surplus arises in the private sector as well as in the public sector. A private firm, however, does not consider consumer surplus, since this accrues to the customer and not to the firm. Unless dual standards are to be applied it may be argued that consumer surplus should not be included in the evaluation of public projects. The consequences of including consumer surplus in public investments while they are not included in private investments may lead to a situation in which it would be easier to justify investment in the public sector than in the private sector. Second, there is some considerable doubt in the view of many economists about the existence and feasibility of measuring the upper regions of the demand curve. This would make it impossible to assess the benefits of a new facility where none existed before and where no "users" can be identified for the period before construction.

On the other hand, the highway engineering definition of benefit, given by equation (2.5),

$$\Delta B^* = V_N (P_M - P_N) \tag{2.5}$$

is conformal with economic theory which states that consumer surplus is part of the net benefit and should be included. The dual standard danger alluded to above may be dismissed on the grounds that there is no clear reason why the public and private sector investments should be evaluated on identical procedures. Indeed, the earlier discussions in this book suggest that commonality of evaluation criteria cannot be obtained, since the private sector is generally concerned with profit maximization to the firm, while the public sector is concerned with welfare maximization. It can clearly be argued that the relevant "profit" for public sector investments is the consumer surplus that accrues to the taxpayer and that, hence, the use of change in consumer surplus as a measure of benefit is wholly appropriate and consistent with private sector evaluation. Potentially, it may be difficult to apply this argument in a developing economy where the problems of identifying users prior to an improvement may preclude the estimation of a prior consumer surplus. With this exception, the authors of this book recommend the use of the highway engineer's definition of benefit as the change in consumer surplus.[10]

So far, the discussion has been concerned with a single facility to be improved. As was mentioned earlier, however, the improvement of any single facility, or the construction of a new facility, will have impacts on other parts of the transportation network. The question that arises here is whether or not to consider the benefits that accrue to users of other facilities. There is much evidence to suggest that these effects should not be ignored and that attempts should be made to include them in the analysis. This, however, requires models capable of giving accurate predictions of the diversions of traffic in a network for some proposed network improvement. Such sophisticated models do not exist at present, and the traditional approach has been to ignore these effects in the evaluation process. This point is dealt with more fully in chapter 6.

The final problem discussed here is the definition of *perceived* user benefit. Two types of user benefit can be defined—perceived and nonperceived. The demand curve is based upon the price of travel as viewed by the traveler. Therefore, it is the perceived price of travel. It is important that care is taken in defining each of perceived and nonperceived costs. Evidence suggests that, as a general rule, the traveler perceives costs as the short-run, or out-of-pocket, costs of each specific trip. For auto users these comprise gasoline, toll, and other trip-associated money outlays, time, discomfort, and inconvenience.

Additional costs are also borne by the auto user, including vehicle ownership, maintenance and repair, accident insurance premiums, garaging (for instance, a house with a garage costs more than one without—hence there is a cost here). These latter costs are generally unperceived costs in that they are not usually considered in relation to any actual trip. Furthermore, these costs are not constituents of the marginal costs of traveling on a specific facility. Clearly, these items should not be included in the analysis even though the user does receive benefit or value from them.

Measurement of Perceived User Price and Benefit

Perceived user benefit and price have now been defined but concern must now focus on the measurement of this in any particular case. It has been established that the price of travel on the demand curve should be the perceived price of travel, and the elements that should enter this have been discussed. The principles underlying the evaluation of benefits for some price change have also been established. A method of computing the volume of travel on a facility must now be introduced. This comprises the determination of the point of intersection of the relevant demand and supply (price-volume) curves.

In order to determine this point of intersection, it is also necessary to ensure that the indices of price for both curves are measured using the same parameters and on the same scales. Thus, both the supply and demand curves must express relationships in terms of the perceived cost of travel. Long-run, nonperceived costs must not be included in the costs for either.

The make-up of the price-volume curve is shown in Figure 2-4. This figure illustrates a probable breakdown of the perceived costs that enter the price-volume relationship. The curve would be for a specific facility, or network, at a specified time, and for a specific trip purpose. Perceived user taxes are based upon an approximate per-mile tax, as is levied through the gasoline tax. Perceived costs and user taxes will not be likely to vary as volume on a facility increases. A congestion-related toll will,

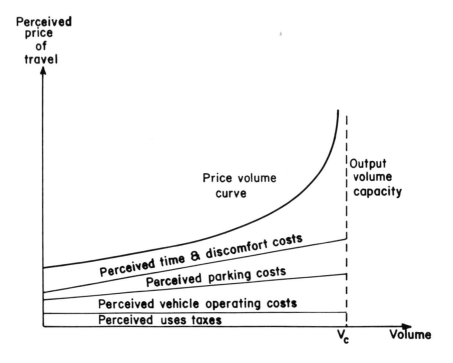

Figure 2-4. Form of the Price-Volume Curve and Perceived Price of Travel.

however, vary with volume. Perceived vehicle-operating costs will tend to increase as volume increases, due principally to higher consumption of gas and oil. Expenditures of time and energy (the latter including concentration, tension, restriction of movement, etc.) will probably increase rapidly as maximum facility capacity is approached. Precisely how rapidly such increases will take place is presently a matter of conjecture. In any case, a price-volume curve of the shape of that shown in Figure 2-4 may be assumed.[11]

When a facility or network is improved, the basic effect will be an increase in capacity. Hence, a new price-volume curve will result, which will probably be lower on the price axis and will become asymptotic to a higher output volume capacity. (This will only occur given the existing methods of charging for highways and mass transport. In the event that new capacity is paid for by increased charges to users, or by a volume-related charge, the price-volume curve would exhibit a different pattern of

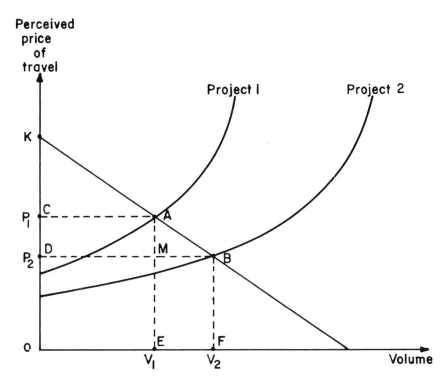

Figure 2-5. Volume Change Resulting from a System Change.

change.) The demand curve, it should be remembered, will be unaffected by the opening of the new facility, ceteris paribus. The position and shape of the demand curve depends only upon the socioeconomic characteristics of the population concerned, and their preference functions. Therefore, if a facility or network, designated Project 1, is changed to a higher capacity facility or network, Project 2, the volumes of use of Project 1 and Project 2, and hence the allowable perceived user benefits of each system, can be computed from Figure 2-5.

It must be remembered that the demand and price-volume curves refer to a specific facility or network at a specific time for one traveler. Alternatively, an assumption is being made that travelers are homogeneous in terms of their preference functions and socioeconomic status, and that travel conditions do not vary significantly over a specific period of time. What would generally be needed for some facility evaluation is an *average* demand curve and an *average* price-volume curve.

24

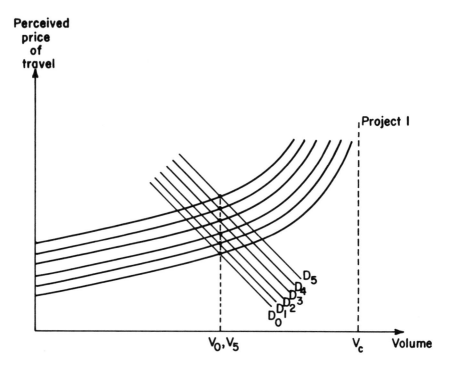

Figure 2-6. Dynamic Changes in Demand and Supply.

Calculation of Project Price and Benefit

In the first chapter mention was made of the problems that exist in evaluating alternatives in a situation where the investment process involves an element of time. The difficulties that arise here stem from two processes. First, there is a tendency for changes to occur in the perceived price of travel. At the present time, the price of travel in terms of true dollars (i.e., after deducting inflation) is rising due to increasing gasoline and oil costs, repair costs, and vehicle ownership costs. Second, there is a tendency for the demand curve to move as a result of changes in real wealth and in social habits. A real growth situation yields a trend for displacement of the demand curve upwards and to the right. These trends can be shown by drawing the demand and price-volume curves for, say, five years at yearly intervals, as shown in Figure 2-6. In this figure, changes in the position of each of the demand and price-volume curves result in a constant travel volume over the time period. At present, this would not be a realistic representation, since the travel volume is actually increasing more rapidly. To simplify the analysis, it is assumed that the units of travel price are

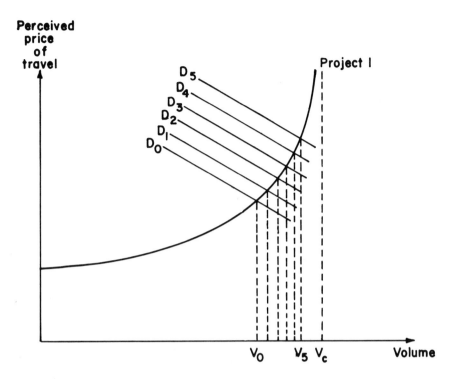

Figure 2-7. Dynamic Demand Shifts for Constant Price-Volume.

adjusted each year to yield the same price-volume curve. This would result in the situation depicted in Figure 2-7. It can now be seen that the increases in travel volume become smaller and smaller, since congestion is being approached more and more rapidly. Clearly, a do-nothing situation will eventually lead to an effectively stable, near-capacity travel volume at a high travel price. Further raising of the demand curve will simply result in a continuing acceptance of rising congestion prices, with no increase or decrease in travel volume. The changes in volume from V_0 to V_5 over five years represent the *normal traffic growth* for the system under consideration, Project 1.

Now, consider the effects of a proposed change in the system, embodied in Project 2. It is assumed that the change represents an improvement in the system. Further, it is assumed that Project 2 will be completed in year 3. The effects may be shown as in Figure 2-8. It would obviously be incorrect to compare perceived benefits in year 0 on both projects, since $P_{2,0}$ and $V_{2,0}$ are hypothetical values unrelated to the system performances that will be achieved under the proposal. Similarly, it would be incorrect to compare Project 1 in year 0 with Project 2 in year 3. Instead,

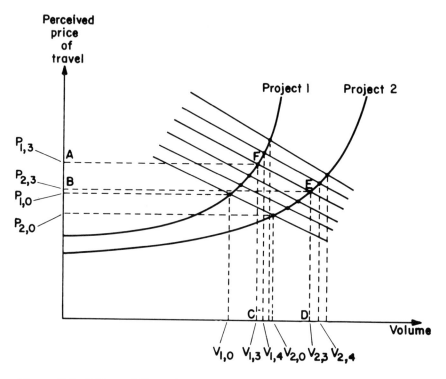

Figure 2-8. Effect of Changing Demand Curve on Evaluation of Benefits.

the initial perceived benefit should be calculated by looking at both systems in year 3. Thus, the change in perceived user benefit resulting from construction of Project 2 is $V_{2,3}(P_{1,3} - P_{2,3})$ or area *ABEF*.

Figure 2-8 also suggests a further factor that needs to be taken into account. Clearly, incremental benefits should not be calculated at a single point in time. In year 3, a volume of traffic, $(V_{2,3} - V_{1,3})$, is induced by the construction of Project 2. However, in year 4, there is a greater difference in volumes $(V_{2,4} - V_{1,4})$ due to a more rapid normal growth in traffic on Project 2 than that on Project 1. Therefore, benefits should be calculated for a period of years, taking into account the differentials in the normal growth rates of the two alternatives. The use of some average travel volume on Project 1 and 2, for an average year in the estimated economic life of the facility, is not to be recommended. In the past, this procedure has led to some serious errors in the computation of benefits. Correctly, the volume of use, and associated prices, should be calculated for each year of the economic life of the facility, and accumulated after allowing for the proper discounting of future benefits. Wohl and Martin [12] detail some errors that have been perpetrated in the past.

A final issue that should be considered here is the point in time at which the benefits should begin to be computed. Again, a diversity of opinion exists. Obviously, in considering the travel benefit, no benefits will accrue from a new system until it is built. On this basis, travel benefit differences between two systems would not be computed until the year in which the new system is operating. Nevertheless, it should be borne in mind that benefits in the future have to be discounted against present losses. In the case of a system that will take upwards of a year to build (including planning, land acquisition, etc.), part of the system costs will be in effect before the system is open. Thus, losses, in terms of investment gains, will be incurred by the resources tied up in construction, while travelers gain no benefit from the new system. This suggests that benefits should be calculated from the point in time at which expenditure on the facility commences. In terms of calculating costs and benefits, the interest losses on resources would then enter as part of the costs during construction.

3

Economic Principles of Interest and Capital Recovery

Considerations of the Time Value of Money

At several points in the preceding chapters, reference has been made to the necessity of determining costs and benefits over a period of time and in the future. For the purposes of evaluation, these costs and benefits must be determined in terms of their worth at the present time. This chapter, therefore, is concerned with the time value of money. The primary concept to be considered here is that the value of money has a temporal dimension. At first sight, this concept may seem strange, since modern society has adopted the monetary unit as a stable measurement of value within the national economy. Even so, a brief consideration of the use of money reveals that it has variable value, within any national economy, with respect to the dimension of time.

Money has little or no intrinsic value of its own (beyond that of the collection of rare coins and the value of the metals used in coinage). Its value lies in those goods and services for which it may be exchanged. Given the uncertainty of life, both from an individual and collective viewpoint, it may be postulated that saving money is a worthless exercise, since it is better to use it to purchase goods and services to be enjoyed in the certain present, rather than to save it for subsequent potential purchase of goods and services in an uncertain future. While this statement represents a wholly plausible and logical (if extreme) outlook, it is, of course, not held constantly by all individuals all of the time. Nevertheless, it does lead to the postulate that the highest value of money is its present value and considered at any time in the future, its value must be less. This may be illustrated readily by considering several situations.

Given a choice between receiving a sum of $10,000 now or in three years' time, virtually everyone would choose to receive it now, all other things being equal. Similarly, if an individual owes $10,000, he would almost always prefer to pay that back in three years' time rather than now, ceteris paribus. Both of these behavior patterns suggest that money has greater value at the present than in the future. Finally, it is extremely unusual for people to hoard money by keeping quantities of coins and notes in some storage location, with the expectation of future spending. Again, the rarity of this behavior further confirms the temporal variation in the value of money.

29

These statements clearly indicate that the values of costs and benefits in the future are not totally determined simply by their monetary values when incurred. Hence, some way must be found to determine the present values of future costs and benefits, in order to permit a realistic evaluation to be undertaken. The question at issue, therefore, is how to discount future costs and benefits in order to determine their present values. The mechanism for this is the discount rate, or interest rate.[1]

The Discount Rate

In order to permit some people and firms to borrow money, the lender must receive additional value in order to be willing to forego present use of his money for purchases of goods and services. In simplest terms, this additional value is the interest on the loan. It, therefore, should represent the rate at which money to be paid in the future is discounted to a present value. Thus, if the lender is willing to offer the borrower $1,000 at an interest rate of 5% per annum, this should imply that the future value of that $1,000 declines at the rate of 5% per annum.

It is not the intent of this text to explore the details of fiscal theory. It should be clear, however, that the system of savings-interest rates, share dividends, loan-interest rates, insurance bonuses, and so forth, are all derived from the simplistic notion put forward in the preceding paragraph. In general, these varying interest rates are different from the actual discount rate at any given time. Interest rates on loans are generally higher than those on savings since the difference represents the income to a savings and loan organization, without which it would not operate. In addition, different types of loans will command differing interest rates, depending upon the security of the loan, i.e., the likelihood that the loan will be fully repaid and the extent to which there is any negotiable security assigned to the institution in exchange for the loan.

The discount rate—and hence interest rates—will vary with the state of the national economy and international trade and monetary situations.[2] Again, it is not appropriate to elaborate on the variation patterns in discount rates. Suffice it to point out that rates are likely to rise in periods of inflation (since people will be likely to be more inclined to spend money at present rather than in the future) and are likely to decline in periods of recession. (Such simple rules do not hold in current international situations, in which inflation and recession or stagnation often occur together.) In general terms, the discount rate will vary with the willingness of people to save, invest, and otherwise defer expenditure to the future.

The discount rate also leads to another concept—that of the "opportunity cost" of money. This opportunity cost is, in fact, the interest (or earnings) that the money could earn if invested or loaned. The question

Table 3-1
Interest Installment Payment Scheme

Year	Interest	Repayment	Outstanding Balance
0	—	—	$1000.00
1	$60.00	$60.00	$1000.00
2	$60.00	$60.00	$1000.00
3	$60.00	$1060.00	0
Total	$180.00	$1180.00	

that must now be addressed is how to calculate the present value of a future sum of money, using the discount rate. This may be calculated by using a *present-worth factor*,[3] shown in equation (3.1).

$$pwf_{i,t} = \frac{1}{(1 + i)^t} \qquad (3.1)$$

This is the rate of discount for a sum of money at the end of the tth year to its equivalent worth at the present time, when the discount rate is i. Clearly, the compounded earnings of a sum of money at rate i for t years is the denominator of equation (3.1). Thus, if the prevailing interest rate is 5%, the present value of $1,000 to be received in three years' time is $863.84. Alternatively, for an individual to be willing to loan $1,000 for three years, he will wish to receive sufficient interest to ensure at least that the present value of the loan and its earnings is $1,000.

When money is borrowed or lent, there are three basic ways in which it may be repaid while providing full present value. First, it may be repaid by paying the interest that has accrued at the end of each year, and repaying the principal in total at the end of each term of the loan. Thus, if $1,000 is borrowed at 6% interest over three years, repayments would be as shown in Table 3-1. In this case, the present value of the loan is determined as shown in equation (3.2).[4]

$$PV = \frac{Pi}{(1 + i)} + \frac{Pi}{(1 + i)^2} + \frac{P + Pi}{(1 + i)^3} \qquad (3.2)$$

where P = principal loaned (i.e., $1,000)

and i = interest rate (i.e., 6%)

Substituting these values in equation (3.2) yields equation (3.3).

$$PV = \frac{60}{1.06} + \frac{60}{(1.06)^2} + \frac{1060}{(1.06)^3} \qquad (3.3)$$

Table 3-2
Equal Installment Payment Scheme

Year	Interest	Repayments	Outstanding Balance
0	—	—	$1000.00
1	$60.00	$374.14	$685.86
2	$41.15	$374.14	$352.87
3	$21.27	$374.14	0
Totals	$122.42	$1122.42	—

Calculating equation (3.3) reveals that the present value is indeed $1,000. Thus, this scheme of repayment guarantees the lender no loss on his money. He realizes the opportunity cost of his money. The second method would be to pay a constant sum each year, comprising interest and principal together. Using the same example, the repayment scheme is shown in Table 3-2. In order to compute the values in Table 3-2, a second concept is needed—the *capital-recovery factor*.[5] This factor permits the computation of the amount of annual payment needed to recover a sum of money in a prescribed period of time and at a given interest rate. The factor is given in equation (3.4).

$$crf_{i,n} = \frac{i(1 + i)^n}{(1 + i)^n - 1} \tag{3.4}$$

In this instance, the present value of the loan is given in equation (3.5).

$$PV = \frac{374.14}{1.06} + \frac{374.14}{(1.06)^2} + \frac{374.14}{(1.06)^3} \tag{3.5}$$

Again, the present value is $1,000, as expected, The third method would be a single payment of interest and principal at the end of the term of the loan. Using the same example, the repayment schedule is shown in Table 3-3. The present value of this loan is shown in equation (3.6). Clearly, the present value is again $1,000.

$$PV = \frac{P(1 + i)^3}{(1 + i)^3} \tag{3.6}$$

Thus, each of the three repayment methods of the example are equivalent in terms of their present worth. This is why each of these methods may be considered equivalent from the point of view of the lender (and also, strictly, of the borrower).

Table 3-3
Single Payment Scheme

Year	Interest	Repayment	Outstanding Balance
0	—	—	$1000.00
1	$60.00	—	$1060.00
2	$63.60	—	$1123.60
3	$67.42	$1191.02	0
Totals	$191.02	$1191.02	—

Table 3-4
Present Worth Factors

Year t	5%	8%	10%
1	0.9524	0.9259	0.9091
2	0.9072	0.8576	0.8264
3	0.8637	0.7938	0.7514
4	0.8226	0.7353	0.6830
5	0.7834	0.6808	0.6208
10	0.6138	0.4634	0.3855
15	0.4809	0.3155	0.2394
20	0.3767	0.2144	0.1486
25	0.2951	0.1462	0.0922
50	0.0871	0.0214	0.0085

The present-worth factor can be used to determine the present worth of any expenditure or benefit at some future time, given the appropriate interest rate. Consider the present value of $100 spent or received at several points in the future, at interest rates of 5, 8, and 10 percent per annum. The present-worth factors are given in Table 3-4. The table illustrates several important points about present worth, time, and interest rates. First, it should be noted that $100 to be received or spent in 50 years' time is currently worth $8.71 at 5% and 85¢ at 10%. Even in 20 years, the $100 is only worth $37.67 or $14.86 at 5% and 10% respectively. Clearly, there is little need to be concerned about costs and benefits that will be incurred more than 20-25 years in the future, at maximum.

Second, the higher the interest rate, the fewer will be the number of years to which calculations will be sensitive. For instance, $100 will be worth $50 in about 13 years at 5%, about 9 years at 8% and in about 7 years at 10%. Thus, the higher the interest rate the greater is the sensitivity to short-term costs and benefits, and the less is the sensitivity to long-term costs and benefits.

Establishing the Discount Rate or Interest Rate

It is clear from the foregoing discussion that the choice of the interest, or discount rate, is of considerable importance in the evaluation process. The ideal would be to use a market discount rate that would be attained in a perfectly competitive economy. This would be determined by the balance between the individual's preference in substituting present consumption for future consumption, and the productivity of alternative investments. However, this ideal rate is very difficult to measure, particularly since the economy is not perfectly competitive. Hence, consideration must be given to the appropriate discount rate as it would be determined from the present economy.

Several matters need to be considered here. First, there is the problem of private and public investment. In considering consumer surplus and other aspects of benefit calculations, certain procedures have been subjected to criticism on the grounds that they would yield dual investment standards for the public sector as compared to private sector. This is clearly an important consideration in arriving at a recommended discount rate for public investment. Attempts at determining a social rate of discount, while being somewhat unsuccessful, would also yield a situation in which a dual standard would exist for the two sectors.

Second, account should be taken of the risks and uncertainties implicit in the analysis.[6] Uncertainties concern the computation of future costs and benefits. The prediction of such values is clearly fraught with errors and these constitute the uncertainty aspect. Ideally, uncertainty should be incorporated by assessing the expected errors on a year-by-year basis, rather than by increasing the discount rate. Risk aversion may be reflected, however, by an increased discount rate. This needs to be taken into account, not by adopting an attitude of risk aversion, but rather by allowing for the existence of a risk aversion premium in the actual market-discount rate. At the same time, care should be taken not to indulge in overoptimism. This is, or has been, a common failing in the public sector, where far too low interest rates have been adopted.

Two final problems of concern are inflation and taxation. It is recommended that the market-discount rate should be adjusted to that value which would be appropriate for a constant value of money, i.e., for neither inflation nor deflation of currency. In general, the market-discount rate will reflect an expectation of inflation or deflation (currently this would be inflation). Under circumstances of expected inflation, the market-discount rate would be reduced to allow for the upward adjustment against continuing inflation. Finally, the market-discount rate is determined by private firms who are subject to taxation of assets and profits. Clearly, the market-discount rate will reflect an allowance for that part of an investment yield that will disappear in taxes. Thus, the private sector balances between the marginal rate of time preference and the *net* productivity of alternative investments. Clearly, the public sector does not consider *net* productivity, but *gross* productivity. Again, this suggests a downward adjustment of the market-discount rate for public investment.

Because of temporal variations in the economy, national differences, and because of the complexities of the preceding arguments, a recommended interest rate cannot be given. In current literature, there seems to be a general agreement that the appropriate discount rate should be in the range of 7-10%. The current public bond market appears to generate rates of around 7¾% for top-rated cities, and higher for those cities that are given lower ratings on bond repayments.

Finally, it should be noted that problems of risk and uncertainty also affect the evaluation processes, apart from their effect on interest rates. Basically, risk, which is the probability that a particular outcome will occur, and uncertainty, which is the state of not knowing the risks, will be of considerable importance in calculating expected costs and benefits. This will not be dealt with here, since it is an extensive subject and impinges greatly upon the actual procedures of decision making.[7] The study of the risk and uncertainty involved in evaluation and decision making may be dealt with using Bayesian statistics.[8] These problems are not considered in this text.

4

The Value of Time Savings

The Need for Time Savings

In chapter 2, the constituent elements of costs and benefits were outlined. Reference to those elements shows that accident reductions and reductions in travel time and cost comprise the direct benefits of most transportation projects. While reductions in accident costs and travel costs (oil, gas, wear and tear, etc.) are significant over the life of the project, they are generally small in relation to total project costs. The most significant element of the benefits is the reduction in user travel times. As a result, the monetization of travel-time savings becomes an important element in the development of an economic-evaluation method for transportation projects.

It should be noted that travel time cannot, in fact, be saved. No form of time can be saved—it can simply be spent in an alternative manner. Therefore, the idea of travel-time savings refers here to a diversion of time that would have been spent in traveling to some other use. The first question to ask is why travel time should have a value? That travel time spent during business hours has a value is obvious, since such time is being paid for by an employer and, therefore, has value or worth to the employer. One can extend this reasoning even further. Since business time spent in traveling is paid for directly, that time is also reflected in the nation's productivity, i.e., in the gross national product (GNP). If travel time of this nature is reduced, then productivity should be increased, thus leading to an increase in GNP, ceteris paribus. Why any time, other than time spent traveling during business hours, should have a value is a more difficult question. A "strict" economic viewpoint[1] would argue that such time does not have value, unless any part of it that is saved is used in productive work. In other words, time has value only when it is used, or may potentially be used, in the production of goods and services. This argument tends to be accepted in nonwestern countries as the correct basis for travel-time valuation and the calculation of transportation project benefits.

The "social viewpoint" holds that any commodity has value if people are willing to trade money (or other commodities of established value) for it. Thus, any travel time has value, if people are found to trade off travel time and money (or another valuable commodity). That people make such trades is self-evident. If they did not, no domestic travel in the United States would be made by air, except for business trips and flying for the sake of flying. Likewise, if the real costs of automobile use were recognized, no one in any of the larger cities with good mass transit would drive downtown to work (or for almost any other purpose). (These statements exclude considerations of other valued attributes, such as comfort. Nevertheless, the presence of differences in these attributes does not invalidate the sense of the statements.) The social value of time that is saved in traveling, as a result of a system improvement, lies in the individual's ability to use that time for some other purpose. The value of such time is related to an individual's perception of what he can do with the time that he saves from travel and the value that he places on that activity. It is in no way related to the GNP, which may also be taken to reflect the inadequacy of GNP as a measure.

A difficulty arises here. The value that an individual places on travel-time savings has been stated as being dependent upon the use to which that time is then put. Clearly, numerous activities are possible as alternatives to spending the time in travel.[2] The analyst, however, is placed in an impossible position, if this requires that time savings be valued on the basis of the alternative uses of that time. First, there are an extremely large number of possible alternative uses that seem unlikely to be responsive to useful aggregation into a few major categories. Second, even if this could be achieved, there is no way to predict how each individual will elect to spend the time that he saves in traveling. Thus, it appears that simplifications of this position must be achieved in order for the valuation of time and its subsequent use in evaluation to be possible.

The remainder of this chapter is concerned with an exploration of these various issues in time evaluation, from both a theoretical and an empirical viewpoint. Before embarking upon this, however, it is important to ascertain the uses to which time values will be put, in order to be able to view the issues in perspective. This is the concern of the next section of this chapter.

Uses of Time Values

There are two primary uses for travel-time values in transportation analysis. The first of these is in economic evaluation of alternative transportation-investment policies, which is the primary concern of this book. The second use, which should not be overlooked, is in the development and application of travel-forecasting and estimating procedures. In this second use, travel-time values have a secondary input into evaluation, since travel-forecasting techniques are used to produce estimates of travel usage for alternative transportation strategies, in both policy and invest-ment. Thus, the value of travel time is used to produce estimates of travel volumes, from which the total travel-time changes are computed. These travel-time changes are multiplied by the value of travel time to yield a substantial portion of the user benefits in the evaluation. Hence, errors in travel-time values are doubly compounded in the process.

As was asserted at the beginning of this chapter, travel-time savings constitute the major portion of the benefits computed in conventional economic evaluations. It has been estimated[3] that 25% of all economic benefits from urban road works in Australia were attributable to private time savings (i.e., travel-time savings other than those accruing to people traveling on business, such as truck drivers, salesmen, etc.). More significantly, between 72% and 81% of the benefits of the United States interstate highway system have been estimated to be derived from travel-time savings.[4] Several other studies show similar results. For the London-Birmingham Motorway,[5] travel-time savings (business and nonbusiness) totalled from 52% to 74% of the benefits, depending upon the value assigned to nonbusiness travel time (from nothing to eight shillings per hour). Foster and Beesley[6] found time savings to represent 48% of the benefits of the Victoria Line in London, while Gillhespy[7] found the time savings on the Tay Road Bridge in Scotland to be 39% of the benefits. In each case, it is clear that the investments could not be justified if travel-time savings were not included. One may conclude from this that the use of travel-time values as a means to determine the monetary benefits of transportation improvements is an essential one in economic evaluation. Further, even if travel-time savings did not constitute a large proportion of the benefits, the travel-time values would still be prominent in the estimation of traffic volumes, from which accident numbers, vehicle-operating costs, etc. are computed as major elements of the non-time-related benefits. Given these facts, some concern with the theory and empiricism of time values appears to be warranted if economic evaluation is considered to be a useful element of an evaluation process.

The Value of Working Time

In the first section of this chapter, two specific types of travel time were identified—working time spent traveling, and nonworking time spent traveling. The issue of valuing working time is much simpler than that of nonworking time for a number of reasons. First, if the definition of travel during working time is applied rigorously, then the value to be defined here is of time that would otherwise be spent working (i.e., producing goods or services). Hence problems alluded to before of the value of the activity that should be substituted for any time saving do not arise here.[8] Second, because the alternative activity to the time saving is work, it appears to be plausible to hypothesize that the value of such travel-time savings will be equal to the opportunity cost of working time. Third, since most working-time travel is paid for by the employer (who will rarely be the traveler) problems of individual idiosyncrasies of choice, perceptual variations on time and cost, and other measurement problems should not arise.

These advantages notwithstanding, the valuation of working time has received relatively little empirical or theoretical research. Strictly speaking, the works of Gronau[9] and DeVany[10] are not valuation of working time values but are studies of values of business time savings and should also be classed with the work of Reichman,[11] who has been concerned with the identification of the time savings for an entire business trip, rather than the difference of schedule times between modes.

Some studies in Britain[12] have attempted to estimate the overhead that should be added to the wage rate, in order to arrive at the value of working-time savings. It appears, however, that these studies have been somewhat unsuccessful, having attempted to determine changes in overhead (for the long run) that result from travel-time savings obtained via transportation-system changes. In other words, the overhead changes (marginal wage increment) have been estimated directly as a change in the plant of the employers resulting from transportation-system improvements.

It seems clear that the value of travel-time savings obtained during working time is equal to the marginal wage rate together with certain overhead costs. These overhead costs must clearly include the payment of fringe benefits that are applied to the employee's base wage and such marginal overheads as the foreman, etc. Whether or not other overhead costs should be added to the wage rate is less clear. Thus, it may be concluded that much work yet remains to be done on the computation of such values of travel-time savings and several theoretical issues remain to be addressed.

The Value of Nonworking Time

On the apparent basis that the valuation of working time is a simple matter that can be disposed of readily, most value-of-time research has concentrated on nonworking time. For example, Hensher[13] lists over forty studies conducted in the last ten years on nonworking travel-time valuation, while the dearth of such research on working-time savings has already been noted. Unlike the situations for working time, there have been extensive studies of both the theoretical base for valuing nonworking travel-time savings and the measurement of values. As was mentioned earlier in this chapter, the basis for valuing nonworking travel-time savings is somewhat controversial, although values have been assigned to such time savings for as much as fifty years.[14] In the next section, several theories of travel-time values are examined, followed by a summary of recent empirical studies on travel-time values.

Some Theories of Travel-Time Valuation

Numerous viewpoints have been put forward about the existence or lack of existence of a value for travel-time savings incurred outside working hours. There is a strong faction which maintains that leisure time can in no way be traded for goods and services and, therefore, has no economic value. The existence of overtime rates of pay has lead at least two researchers to diametrically opposite opinions about the existence or nonexistence of a value of private travel-time savings.[15] On the one hand, it is argued that higher rates of pay for overtime than for regular working time imply that leisure time has a considerable value to the individual, possibly being as high as or higher than those overtime rates. On the other hand, it has also been argued that both the eagerness shown by workers to obtain their share of overtime, and the insistence in agreements to reduce working hours that the weekly wage should be unchanged reinforce the fact that little value is placed on leisure time and a high price is placed on effort. In spite of this, it is generally considered that travel time spent during the leisure hours should indeed be attributed a value and that this value should be taken into consideration in an economic analysis of alternative transportation plans.

Most of the early measurement work was based on very little theory. Although measurements began in the early 1940s, the theory consisted of a simple statement, relating to choices of route in highway travel. This statement was that values of travel time could be inferred from studies of choices that comprised a faster, more expensive route (e.g., a toll bridge) and a slower, cheaper route (e.g., a free bridge reached by detour).[16] Although the empirical studies became more sophisticated, no attempts were made to develop a clear theoretical statement of value of travel time until late in the 1960s. (The empirical work is discussed later in this chapter.)

In the late 1960s, several theoretical statements of the value of travel-time savings for nonworking time were put forward.[17] While it is not possible to detail each of these theories here, that of de Donnea[18] is interesting to examine, since it also raises specific questions about the effects of attributes other than cost and time. In this derivation, the utility of a consumer, for the joint product of an activity and the travel required to undertake that activity, is considered. The utility function is defined by equation (4.1).

$$U = U[A_i, G(t_i, X_{ki})] \quad i = 1, \ldots, I; \quad k = 1, \ldots, K \qquad (4.1)$$

where A_i = level of ith activity ($i = 1, \ldots, I$)

X_{ki} = the quantity of good or service k used in the production of activity $i(k = 1, \ldots, K)$

t_i = the time used in the production of activity i

$G(\ )$ = the satisfaction or dissatisfaction that proceeds from the circumstances under which the time used to produce activity i is spent

The level of the ith activity is itself a function of the time used in the production of the activity and the quantity of goods and services (X_{ki}) needed for its production.

Three assumptions are necessary to proceed. First, it is assumed that the individual consumer cannot adjust the length of his working time according to his preferences. Thus, the amounts of time for work activities and for all nonwork activities are assumed fixed. Second, it is assumed that, in the classical economics approach, the consumer will choose to maximize his utility, subject to income and time constraints. Finally, it is necessary to assume that the consumer has no other income than his wage or salary. In order to formalize the theory, the constraints on utility maximization must be specified in mathematical terms. Given the assumption on nonvariability of working time and the limitation on income, these constraints are given by equations (4.2), (4.3) and (4.4).

$$Y = \sum_{k=1}^{K} \sum_{i=1}^{I} p_k X_{ki} \qquad (4.2)$$

where Y = income in a given period

p_k = market price of good or service k

X_{ki} = quantity of good or service k required for the production of activity i

$$T_c = \sum_{i=1}^{I} t_i \qquad (4.3)$$

where T_c = total consumption of time in a given period

$$T_c = T - T_w \qquad (4.4)$$

where T = total time in a given period (e.g., 24 hours in a day)

T_w = total work time in a given period

Given these statements of the constraints, the utility can be maximized by the procedure of Lagrange multipliers, as shown in equation (4.5)

$$V = U[A_i, G(t_i, X_{ki})] + \lambda \left[Y - \sum_k \sum_i p_k X_{ki} \right]$$

$$+ \mu \left[T_c - \sum_i t_i \right] \qquad (4.5)$$

where λ, μ = Lagrange multipliers.

It is not necessary to define the utility function in order to develop the theory. It is only necessary to remember that A_i is a function of t_i and X_{ki}. The first derivatives of equation (4.5) with respect to t_i and X_{ki}, set equal to zero for maximization, are shown in equations (4.6) and (4.7).

$$\frac{\delta U}{\delta A_i} \frac{\delta A_i}{\delta X_{ki}} + \frac{\delta U}{\delta G} \frac{\delta G}{\delta X_{ki}} - \lambda p_k = 0 \qquad (4.6)$$

$$\frac{\delta U}{\delta A_i} \frac{\delta A_i}{\delta t_i} + \frac{\delta U}{\delta G} \frac{\delta G}{\delta t_i} - \mu = 0 \qquad (4.7)$$

These two equations represent a system of equations for all i and all k.

Since X_{ki} is the quantity of a good or service k required for the production of activity i, and A_i designates the level of the activity i, it follows that the first term of equation (4.6) is the marginal utility of a good or service k that results from its marginal productivity in the production of an activity i. The second term of equation (4.6) is the marginal utility of a good or service k that results from the impact of the quantity of that good or service used on the circumstances under which the time input of activity i must be spent. Since both these terms are marginal utilities, then λp_k must also be a marginal utility. Hence, λ is the marginal utility of money.

Equation (4.6) may thus be interpreted in the following manner. The total marginal utility of a good or service k used in the production of an activity i is equal to its price p_k multiplied by the marginal utility of money.

In a similar examination of equation (4.7), it is apparent that μ is the marginal utility of time, which is the same in all consumption activities. The marginal utility of time is also seen, from equation (4.7), to be the sum of marginal utility of time as an input in the production of activity i and of the marginal satisfaction or dissatisfaction that results from the circumstances in which the time is spent in producing activity i.

Following de Donnea's notation, equations (4.6) and (4.7) can be simplified. Let

$$\frac{\delta U}{\delta G} \frac{\delta G}{\delta X_{ki}} = g_{ki}$$

and

$$\frac{\delta U}{\delta G} \frac{\delta G}{\delta t_i} = g_{ti}$$

Equations (4.6) and (4.7) may be rewritten as equations (4.8) and (4.9), respectively.

$$\frac{\delta U}{\delta A_i} \frac{\delta A_i}{\delta X_{ki}} = \lambda p_k - g_{ki} \tag{4.8}$$

$$\frac{\delta U}{\delta A_i} \frac{\delta A_i}{\delta t_i} = \mu - g_{ti} \tag{4.9}$$

Dividing equation (4.8) by (4.9) provides a definition of dt_i/dX_{ki}, which is the rate of substitution of time and a given input k used in the production of activity i. This is shown in equation (4.10).

$$-\frac{dt_i}{dX_{ki}} = \frac{\lambda p_k - g_{ki}}{\mu - g_{ti}} \tag{4.10}$$

The marginal value of time is given by equation (4.11).

$$\frac{\mu - g_{ti}}{\lambda} = \frac{dX_{ki}}{dt_i} (p_k - g_{ki}/\lambda) \tag{4.11}$$

In words: the marginal value of time used as input in given activity i is equal to the rate of technical substitution of an input k of activity i and of time (multiplied by) the difference between the price p_k of the input k and the marginal value of the effect of input k on the circumstances under which the whole time required to produce activity i must be spent.[19]

When the circumstances under which time is spent are ignored, the marginal value of time would be defined as in equation (4.12).

$$\frac{\mu - 1_i}{\lambda} = -\frac{dx_{ki}}{dt_i} p_k \tag{4.12}$$

where $\quad 1_i = (\delta U/\delta L)(\delta L/\delta t_i)$

$\quad L(t_i) =$ satisfaction or dissatisfaction that derives from the circumstances under which time is spent, independent of the goods or services

In general, the values of time derived in past studies have been based on equation (4.12), whereas they should have been based on equation (4.11).

Three important conclusions may be drawn from this derivation. First, the value of travel time or of time spent in any other activity can clearly be seen to exist, thus responding to the criticism that the only time that has value is that used in production activities. Second, it is apparent that the value of a travel-time saving is dependent, in fact, upon the activity that replaces travel. Third, it is very clear that the value of travel time (as opposed to a time saving) is a function of the circumstances under which that time is spent, i.e., the comfort and amenities experienced in travel. Thus, it is clear that *all* attributes of travel must be taken into account when deriving values of travel time.

Other theories of value of time[20] do not depart from the major points of de Donnea, although they introduce some variations on the precise assumptions necessary and the form of the value of time, per se. Watson[21] for example, chooses to avoid the construct of the circumstances under which time is spent and derives a simple time-cost trade-off model. This arises from a simplistic assumption that the only "good" used in the production of a trip is the monetary cost. De Donnea argues, more correctly, that other "goods" are also involved, such as comfort, effort, etc. In effect, Watson's time value is closer to equation (4.12) and supports the more traditional view of time valuation studies.

The Measurement Dilemma

Traditional Measurement Techniques

While economic theory clearly shows that nonworking time spent in any activity, including travel, has value, the theory does not specify how this value should be measured. The traditional (pretheory) approach was to find trade-off situations that faced travelers and derive values of time from measurements of the trade off. One such typical situation was a toll road-free road choice. In general, the value of time was defined as shown by equation (4.13).

$$V = \frac{O\Delta m}{\Delta t} \qquad (4.13)$$

where V = value of travel time

O = operating costs per mile

Δm = additional distance required to save time

Δt = time saving of the faster alternative

In the event that the faster alternative also involved the payment of a toll, the equation was modified to (4.14).

$$V = \frac{f + O\Delta m}{\Delta t} \qquad (4.14)$$

where f = toll paid

Subsequent measurement was based on somewhat more sophisticated considerations of the traveler's choice situation. In this work, models were constructed of the choice process between alternative modes or routes of travel, such as that shown in equation (4.15).

$$p_m = \frac{\exp G(X_m)}{\sum_k \exp G(X_k)} \qquad (4.15)$$

where $\quad p_m$ = probability of (or proportion) choosing alternative m

$$G(X_m) = \alpha_0 + \sum_t \alpha_t X_{tm}$$

X_{tm} = characteristics of alternative m

α_0, α_1, etc. = coefficients found from revealed behavior

In the case of two alternatives, equation (4.15) can be rewritten in terms of differences in characteristics of the alternatives, as shown in equation (4.16).

$$p_m = \frac{1}{1 + \exp G(X_n - X_m)} \qquad (4.16)$$

Considering the situation in which $G(X_k)$ is defined in terms of travel time and travel cost alone, the term $G(X_n - X_m)$ of equation (4.16) becomes equation (4.17).

$$G(X_n - X_m) = \alpha_0 + \alpha_1(t_n - t_m) + \alpha_2(c_n - c_m) \qquad (4.17)$$

The ratio of the coefficients of time and cost indicates the comparative importances of cost and time in the revealed behavior situation. Hence, the ratio has been interpreted, in many studies, as the "value of travel time." The value of travel time is, thus, given by equation (4.18) in these studies.

$$V = \frac{\hat{\alpha}_1}{\hat{\alpha}_2} \qquad (4.18)$$

All of these methods have several problems in common. First, none of them take into account de Donnea's concept of the circumstances under which the time is spent. The only method with the potential for doing this is the choice model of equation (4.15), where the $G(X)$ function may include terms relating to comfort, scenic appeal, etc. Thus, if terms of relative comfort *com* and scenic appeal *sa* are added to the function, equation (4.17) becomes equation (4.19).

$$G(X_n - X_m) = \alpha'_0 + \alpha'_1(t_n - t_m) + \alpha'_2(c_n - c_m)$$

$$+ \alpha'_3(com_n - com_m) + \alpha'_4(sa_n - sa_m) \qquad (4.19)$$

The coefficient ratio, previously described as the value of time is now the ratio of the newly established coefficients, as shown in equation (4.20).

$$V = \frac{\hat{\alpha}'_1}{\hat{\alpha}'_2} \qquad (4.20)$$

This value will be correct, in terms of de Donnea's theory, if and only if the two variables describe fully the circumstances under which the travel time is spent that differ between the alternatives m and n. The earlier methods cannot take this concept into account.

Second, none of the methods offers any possibility for statistical assessment of the resulting value. Although the coefficients, α_1 and α_2, may be normally distributed, the ratio of two such variables is most unlikely to be normally distributed, or indeed to have any regular distribution that might permit some form of statistical testing.[22] Indeed, it can be shown that the underlying distribution of the value of time, when derived from a coefficient ratio, is usually highly skewed and somewhat irregular.[23] In the case of the toll facility-free facility trade-off models, there are no known underlying distributions and even less likelihood of being able to structure formal statistical tests.

The third and most telling problem lies with the definition of what is being measured from these studies. In all of the studies, the V of equations (4.13), (4.14), (4.18), and (4.20) is labeled the value of time. Two principal questions arise: Is this an average or a marginal value? and, Is it a value of time at all? An increasing number of transportation researchers and professionals are becoming convinced that V is not a value of time at all. In order to examine this dilemma more closely, definitions of the marginal and average values of time are necessary. For working purposes the following definitions are put forward:

The marginal value of time is the amount of money that an individual is willing to pay to save one additional minute of travel time, or it is the inverse of the amount of time he is willing to pay to save one additional unit of money (e.g., one cent) at the margin.

The average value of time is the ratio of the total amount of money that an individual is willing to pay to purchase a given time saving, or it is the inverse of the ratio of the amount of time that an individual is willing to pay to purchase a given monetary saving.

Bearing these definitions in mind, we see that the methods described in this section do not measure either the average or the marginal value of time. All of the observations on which the values are based concern the amount of money that an individual must pay for a time saving or the amount of time that he must pay for a cost saving. Neither measure ascertains the willingness to pay, *unless the traveler is at the margin*. In fact, it can be asserted that the toll road-free road measures (equations (4.13) and (4.14)) are average *prices* of time and are not *values* of time.

In the case of the choice model, further complications enter. First, it is clear that a number of those travelers observed in a choice situation will have a "dominant" alternative and an "inferior" alternative. A dominant alternative is one for which both the cost and time are less than for any other alternative, while an inferior alternative is one which is both more expensive and slower than any other alternative. Given that the specification of the choice process for most individuals will be incomplete, it follows that some travelers will be observed choosing the inferior alternative (presumably because it has other attributes that make it attractive), while many of those who have a dominant alternative will choose it. For each of these groups of people, the price of time is negative. The coefficients of travel time and travel cost in the choice model are derived from effectively averaging the prices of time of each individual. Thus, the choice models also produce an average price of time, including averaging across dominant and inferior alternatives.

Several additional properties of the choice-model estimates are worth noting. First, the choice models can take account of the effects of the circumstances under which the time is spent. This is done through the inclusion of additional attribute variables in the model. Insofar as these variables are even partially correlated with either cost or time, the coefficients of cost and time will be changed in value, generally leading to a reduction in the estimated average price of time. Second, an unique average price of time can only be obtained from a choice model that is formulated in terms of attribute differences. (A model based upon any form of ratios will yield a continuum of values of the average price of time, varying with amounts of time and cost involved.) This also suggests that the coefficient ratio may approximate a marginal price of time, since the value is obtained from the differences of time and costs, i.e., the excess or marginal cost and time differences. Third, the relationship between choices, the price of time, and income can be investigated through the choice models by several techniques.[24] These include stratification by income, use of income in combination with either cost or time in the model, and use of income as an additive variable. In the last case, the effect of the income variable is only to modify the coefficient values, and variations in the price of time do not occur with income. By and large, it may be postulated that higher prices of time would be likely to be associated with higher incomes for trips undertaken on a regular basis, while the average price may show little or no consistent variation for infrequent trips. This postulate is based upon the assumption that households will tend to locate and make trip choices that are conformal with their income and the marginal utilities of all activities that are undertaken on a regular basis. Fourth, it becomes clear that situations can arise in which the price of time is determined as being negative. This will occur for a sample that comprises largely dominant-alternative choosers and inferior-alternative choosers, where the former outnumber the latter substantially. Indeed, in such a case, the coefficient of travel cost difference is likely to be statistically insignificant since it will not correlate highly with choice.

From these various points, it may be concluded that the price of time is also a purely descriptive variable. It is derived from and describes a specific choice situation. The average, or marginal average price of time depends upon the mix of time and cost trade-off situations in the data sample and the extent of the existence of dominant and inferior alternatives. Should any of these elements change (in a predictive scenario) so will the average price of time change and, with it, the behavioral response of the population group.

In summary, traditional methods of measurement have led, without exception, to the estimation of a price of time rather than a value of time. This price of time is, furthermore, situation specific and cannot be used as a basis for evaluation. The extent to which the choice models can be considered to be more than descriptive models is also questionable.

Some Alternative Measurement Techniques

It is apparent from the preceding discussion that the required measurement technique should be based upon a determination of willingness to pay. At least two alternative procedures have been put forward to permit the estimation of values of travel time. In this section, each of these techniques is examined.

The first and most logical procedure is to attempt to determine how much money individuals are willing to pay to save time (and vice versa) at the margin. Such a procedure was utilized by Hensher.[25] Essentially, this technique involves asking people how much of a change in the cost of their present or alternative travel modes would be necessary to cause them to change their choice of mode. Accurately answered, such a question should yield estimates of the marginal value of time of each individual.

The primary problem that arises from this measurement technique is centered around the request for people to indicate their anticipated behavior under hypothetical circumstances. There is much evidence to suggest that people cannot estimate well how they will behave under such hypothetical situations. Primarily, people are less aware of the extent of their own inertia against change than they need to be, in order to indicate the extent of the monetary change necessary to cause them to change their choice of either mode or route. Assuming, however, that such information can be supplied by the individual, the choice equation is modified to equation (4.21).[26]

$$G(X_A - X_C) = \beta_0 + \beta_1(t_A - t_C) + \beta_2(c_A - c_C + TP_C) \qquad (4.21)$$

where TP_c = the transfer payment on the chosen mode or route

t_A, c_A = time and cost by the alternative mode or route

t_c, c_C = time and cost by the chosen mode or route

However, the inclusion of the transfer payment TP_C makes the traveler indifferent between his usual and alternative choices. In the probability model of equation (4.16), the point of indifference is given by a probability of 0.5, which occurs only when $G(X_A - X_C)$ is zero. Hence, equation (4.21) can be rewritten as equation (4.22).

$$(c_A - c_C + TP_C) = \gamma_0 + \gamma_1 (t_A - t_C) \qquad (4.22)$$

The coefficient γ_1 is now a direct estimate of the marginal value of time. Clearly, equation (4.22) can be extended to include other attribute differences, thus taking into account the circumstances under which travel time is spent. Likewise, the effect of income and other socioeconomic variables can again be taken into account through the various strategies of interactive variables, stratification, and the addition of socioeconomic variables.[27]

Currently, the only significant problem in this approach is the measurement of the transfer payment. Direct questioning appears to have serious problems since individuals probably do not know where their indifference point is until they experience it. It might be possible to estimate values of time for a group, using direct measurement, provided that certain distributional assumptions were met. Primarily, it would be necessary for there to be a symmetrical distribution of travelers around the indifference point with respect to cost advantages and cost disadvantages. In this case, it may be assumed that the underestimates below and above the indifference point would cancel out to produce a reasonably accurate average marginal value of travel time. Alternatively, it is necessary to seek out methods of determining the transfer payment without resorting to direct enquiry. Techniques from psychological measurement may supply the desired methodology, but experimentation on this has not been undertaken so far.

The second method is based upon a similar concept to that of willingness to pay, but examines revealed choices and requires no other additional information than the perceived attributes of the alternatives that are the subject of the choice process. With respect to willingness to pay, this technique is restricted to those individuals who are "traders." A trader is defined as an individual who is in the position of trading off a disadvantage in one or more attributes for an advantage in one or more other attributes. It must be stressed that being a trader or not, in any choice situation, is a function of the choice situation and is not a personal characteristic.

For example, an individual may face a choice between automobile and transit, where the costs and times for a specific trip are as follows:

$$\text{Automobile} \quad : \quad \text{cost} = 55\cancel{c}; \quad \text{time} = 35 \text{ minutes}$$

$$\text{Transit} \quad : \quad \text{cost} = 35\cancel{c}; \quad \text{time} = 45 \text{ minutes}$$

Assuming that only time and cost are important, the individual who faces this situation is, ipso facto, a trader. A second individual may face the following situation:

$$\text{Automobile} \quad : \quad \text{cost} = 40\cancel{c}; \quad \text{time} = 30 \text{ minutes}$$

$$\text{Transit} \quad : \quad \text{cost} = 45\cancel{c}; \quad \text{time} = 45 \text{ minutes}$$

This individual, given the same assumption as before, is not a trader. Clearly, in both cases, the situation that is faced determines the status of either being or not being a trader.

The estimation technique, which is originally due to Beesley[28], is concerned with an analysis of traders alone. The postulate is that anyone who does not face a trading situation also does not reveal any information about his value of travel time. The technique can best be described by a consideration of the situation in which only cost and time are relevant attributes of choice. (The technique is readily extended to multi-attribute situations, as is described later.) Under these circumstances, traders are those individuals who face two alternatives such that one alternative is faster and more expensive and the other is slower and cheaper. All individuals, whether traders or not, can be located on a two-dimensional plot, on which the axes are travel time difference (Δt) and travel cost difference (Δc), as shown in Figure 4-1. Differences in travel time and travel cost are determined as the difference between alternative (or not usual) and chosen (or usual) mode of travel.

Quadrant I defines those individuals with a dominant choice (i.e., the chosen option is both faster and cheaper). These individuals are not trad-

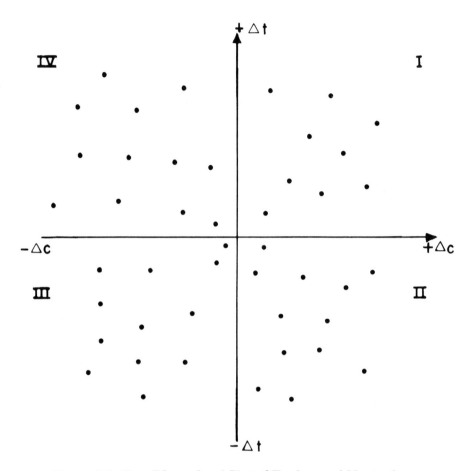

Figure 4-1. Two-Dimensional Plot of Traders and Nontraders.

ers and do not contribute to the analysis at this point. Individuals in quadrant III have selected an "illogical" choice, ceteris paribus, and are also nontraders for the present. Quadrant II defines a group of traders who are *cost preferrers*, i.e., they prefer to sacrifice time to save money. Quadrant IV defines a second group of traders, who are *time preferrers*. Thus, it is argued that only the data points in quadrants II and IV are relevant for this analysis.

As discussed before, only a traveler who is at the margin exhibits his value of travel time by the choice that he makes. Since it is not possible to determine who is at the margin, it must be assumed a priori that nobody is. Those individuals who are cost preferrers show that they are willing to sacrifice an observed number of minutes for the observed cost saving. The ratio of the cost saving to the time sacrifice would be the value of time for the individual, were he or she at the margin. It is useful to consider a specific example. Using the earlier trading example, the cost preferrer would choose transit, so electing a 10 cent cost savings at the price of a 10 minute disadvantage. If the cost preferrer were at the margin, his value of time would be 60 cents per hour. It may be postulated that his value of time is no greater than this, but could be less. If his value of time were greater, say 66 cents per hour, he would choose auto, rather than transit, since this value implies that the individual would need to save at least 11 cents on transit for a 10 minute time loss. Hence, it is inconsistent. However, his value of time could be less and still be consistent with a trade-off of 10 minutes time loss for a 10 cent saving. Suppose that the individual has a value of time of 45 cents per hour. He would be willing to trade 10 minutes for a 7 1/2 cent cost saving. Since he actually achieves a 10 cent cost saving, he receives a 2 1/2 cent consumer surplus. In like manner, the time preferrer demonstrates a lower bound on his time value, in terms of the choice he is observed to make. Thus, if he chose auto in the above example, it can be stated that his value of time is at least 60 cents per hour. If his value of time were $1.20 per hour, he values the 10 minute time saving at 20 cents, but only has to pay 10 cents for it, thus achieving a 10 cent consumer surplus. Clearly, a transit choice would not be consistent for this traveler.

Now, it is necessary to consider how values of time can be inferred from the data of cost-time trade-offs of the traders in quadrants II and IV, in Figure 4-2. The line OA has a slope of 10 cents/20 minutes (or a "value" of time of 30 cents per hour). This is the upper bound value of individual A. Likewise, OB has a slope of 20 cents/10 minutes (or a "value" of time of $1.20 per hour), which is a lower bound for individual B. In both quadrants, individuals near the vertical, or Δt, axis have very low values of time and those near the horizontal, or Δc, axis have very high values of time.

In quadrant II, the line OC represents a consistent value of time for all observations in that quadrant. Everyone in that quadrant exhibits an upper bound on their value of time. This line is approximately 12 cents an hour. The two observations on the line have this as an upper bound value. All other observations have a higher upper bound. Hence, OC is consistent for this quadrant. Likewise, the line OD is consistent with all observations in quadrant IV, representing a value of $3.00 per hour. Again, this line passes through the observations exhibiting the maximum lower bound in the quadrant. These two situations are shown in Figures 4-3 and 4-4, where the Xs are sample points from Figure 4-2. All that is known for quadrant II samples (Figure 4-3) is that their value of time lies between the exhibited value (from the observed choice) and zero. The line OC clearly intersects all observations within their known range of values.

In Figure 4-4, the known ranges of value of time are between the ex-

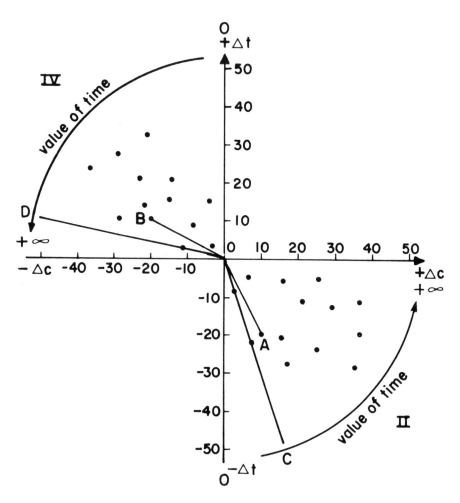

Figure 4-2. Value of Time Inference from Plot of Traders.

hibited value and infinity. Again, the line *OD* intersects all observations within their known range of values and is, therefore, consistent.

The question may now be posed as to why two different values should be found in the two quadrants. Just as the state of being a trader or not is a function of the choice situation being faced by an individual, so the state of being a cost preferrer or time preferrer is a function of the choice situation modified by the true value of time of the individual. Thus, there is no a priori reason to suppose that the values of time, for a reasonably homogeneous sample of time preferrers and cost preferrers, should be different for the two quadrants. As a consequence, it would seem to be more rea-

55

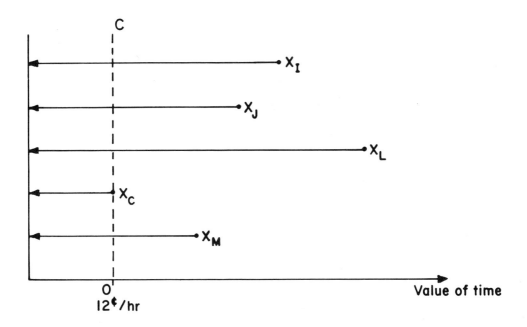

Figure 4-3. Values of Time for Quadrant II Samples.

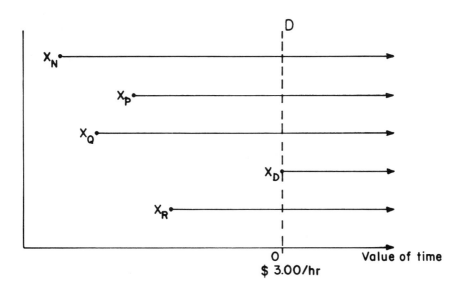

Figure 4-4. Values of Time for Quadrant IV Samples.

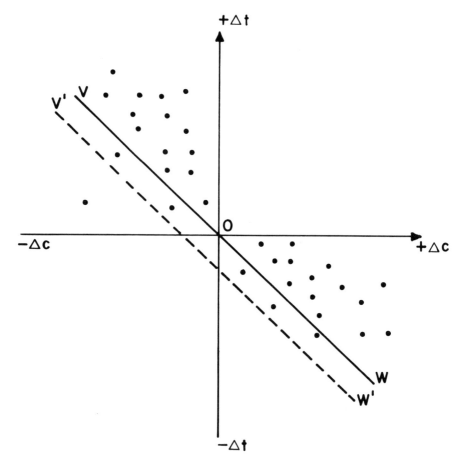

Figure 4-5. Determination of Value of Time from Trader Plot.

sonable to estimate a single value of time for both quadrants. It is clear that, since one quadrant gives upper-bound information and the other lower-bound information, a single value that is consistent with all observations is unlikely to exist.

To determine a value of time by this method, it is necessary to find the line, through the origin, that jointly misclassifies (i.e., is inconsistent with) the minimum possible number of individuals. This is shown in Figure 4-5 by the line VW. It should be noted that, in both quadrants, the misclassified individuals are those below the line (where Δt is on the vertical axis and Δc on the horizontal axis).[29] It is also important to note that, because each individual indicates only a bound on his time value, the distance of misclassified observations from the value-of-time line is irrelevant.

One should consider the question of why the value-of-time line should pass through the origin of the time-cost plot. For example, the line $V'W'$ appears to be more desirable, since it yields the same time value as VW but misclassifies only one, as opposed to six, observations. It is clear, however, that this is illusory. The value of time for any observation in the figure is determined from the slope of the line that joins the origin, 0, to the observation. Hence, although the line $V'W'$ has fewer points below it, the value it represents is still inconsistent with the five points below VW. Thus, it can be asserted that the joint minimum misclassification line must pass through O.

Two additional questions must also be addressed. First, this misclassification method is correct only when there are equal numbers of cost preferrers and time preferrers. If there were more time preferrers than cost preferrers, the line would tend to be weighted towards the lower bound "best-fit" line, and vice versa. In general, however, there will be unequal numbers in the two trader groups. This requires a weighting procedure for the points in one of the quadrants, such that each quadrant has an equal weight in determining the location of the best-fit line. Second, though the line has been referred to as a best-fit line, this is determined through a simple counting procedure. Thus, there is no statistical validation of the value of time and no means for determining statistical confidence limits on the value. Nevertheless, the values determined from this technique appear to come as close to being true values of travel time as any method can produce.

A final point to be made on this technique relates to the accounting for socioeconomic characteristics and other attributes of the alternative choices. The effects of both sets of characteristics can be examined through stratification. This technique is quite straightforward for socioeconomic characteristics. For example, a given population can be stratified by income, and separate plots made for each income group. Separate values of time can be determined for each group and compared to see if there are apparent real differences. Again, however, it must be noted that no significance tests are available for comparing values from different strata.

The process for accounting for other attributes is a little more complex. Assuming that complete specification and measurement of attributes has been achieved, it may be argued that a "true" value of time will be exhibited only by those who have no advantages or disadvantages on any other attributes than time and cost for one alternative compared with the other. These are the cost-time traders. All other people are either nontraders or are trading some combination of attributes for some second, different combination of attributes. It may be postulated that estimates of the same value of time will be increasingly deflated as other attributes increase, and may also be less reliably estimated due to the varying effects of these other attributes. Values of the other attributes may be derived through an iterative process, in which apparent nontraders successively become traders by estimating values of the various attributes.

An example is desirable to clarify the process. Suppose that two alternative modes of travel—auto and bus—are completely specified by three variables: time, cost, and convenience. A set of observations has been obtained on a group of travelers, for all of whom the chosen mode has been established, together with the values of time, cost, and convenience for each alternative. Values of time difference, cost difference, and convenience difference are computed for each individual, where the difference is expressed as the value on the alternative minus the value on the chosen mode. If value of travel time only is of interest then the procedure is to identify those traders who have a zero convenience difference and estimate the value of time from those observations. If the value of convenience is now desired, a new travel "cost" difference is computed for every observation by multiplying the travel-time difference by the estimated value of time and adding it to the cost difference. A new trader plot is now constructed of convenience difference against "cost" difference. Since this plot represents joint trade-offs of cost and time against convenience, cost and convenience against time, and time and convenience against cost, many of the previous nontraders will now emerge as traders. The value of convenience can then be estimated.

Theoretically, this process should be totally reversible, in that the value of convenience could be estimated first, followed by the value of time estimated from the augmented trader set. The reversibility of this process has not been tested empirically. The process can be repeated for as many attributes as are needed to specify the choice between alternatives.

Concluding Comments on Measurement

It appears to be clear that the traditional methods of measurement estimate an average price of time, rather than an average or marginal value of time. Thus, estimation of "values" from toll-free travel choices or from choice models for mode or route does not produce values of travel time. Indeed, it has been argued that the requirements and goals of travel-choice modeling are incompatible with those of value of time estimation.[30]

In order to estimate values of time (either average or marginal) it appears to be necessary to confine analysis to traders, or to place everyone in the position of trading at the margin. While both of these techniques have drawbacks (lack of statistical tests for trader analysis; difficulty of measuring the transfer payment for marginal analysis), they appear to be the most promising techniques for estimating time values. Both techniques need further research and empirical refinement before reliable values can be considered to have been achieved.

A final comment is in order concerning the estimation of true marginal or average values of time. At no point has the question been addressed of whether a true value of time is desired for evaluation purposes. It is clear that the use of a value of time will necessitate determining who will be traders and who will not under any given policy or investment alternative that is to be considered. The use of an average price of time is incorrect, however, since this is a function of the proportion of traders and the system that exists. Thus, the traditional use of average prices of time is clearly incorrect. The use of values of time presents serious analytical demands, however, that may not be possible to meet.

A second aspect of this issue relates to the equity of decisions based upon the use of correct values of time. If values of time increase with increasing income, then maximum benefits are likely to accrue from investments or policies that save most time for the highest income groups and least for the lowest income groups. This is clearly an inappropriate decision from a public investment viewpoint. The issue has not been resolved and appears to be a fundamental one in the use of economic evaluation. A more detailed discussion of this issue is to be found later in this book.

Historical Summary of Time Values

Although the previous section has raised some very serious questions about the estimation of time values, benefit estimation using some form of "value of time" has been used in transportation for more than fifty years. It is quite appropriate, therefore, to review some of the values that have been used, the methods by which they have been estimated, and the sources of the values. Two extensive reviews have been published previously,[31] and a detailed review of all such values is not appropriate here. Rather, an attempt is made to highlight some of the landmark values that have been used.

The earliest value of time that appears to be reported in the literature is an assumed value of $3.00 an hour in 1925,[32] determined by the Bureau of Public Roads. This value was applied to all vehicles and appears to be the highest value assumed or measured until a 1960 study by Hummel[33] gave $4.80 for an urban car and $4.11 for a rural car. This value of $4.80 an hour is the highest value in the 45 years from 1925 through 1970. For the period from 1925 until 1961, the value of time averages about $1.26 an hour, with variations from a low of 30¢ to the high of $4.80. The majority of values in this period were assumed without empirical evidence. The most common values were 60¢ per vehicle-hour and $1.20 per vehicle-hour. Both of these values appeared first in 1931 and resulted from empirical measurements.[34] None of the studies through 1961 used anything other than either toll free choices or freeway/street choices for deriving values of travel time for nonworking time.

The most notable aspect of the values of time for the period through 1961 is the wide variety of values and the lack of consistency in the methods by which they were derived. As a result of this situation (a mean value of $1.26 per vehicle hour and standard deviation of 94¢), the Bureau of Public Roads contracted to Stanford Research Institute (SRI) in 1961 for a major study of the value of time for passenger cars (traveling in nonworking time). The final report of the study was published in 1967,[35] and a further contract was given to SRI to examine several further questions surrounding value of time. This work was published primarily in 1970.[36]

The approach taken by SRI was similar to the conventional toll-free approach, in that it was based upon observations of motorists who were in a position to choose between a toll road and a free road. As far as possible, the toll-free choices were selected such that the two alternative routes were almost indistinguishable from each other in terms of everything except travel time, distance, and cost. The similarity to the early studies ends at this point. The value of time was estimated from the structuring of choice models, in terms of travel times. Thus, the value of time was inferred from a ratio of coefficients of cost and time difference variables in a choice model, fitted on the basis of revealed preferences.

Two sets of measurements were collected. First, travel times and travel costs were measured through engineering techniques to establish a set of objective values for each traveler. This was done by determining, from a sample of travelers at each site, the route used, timing the trip by multiple runs using a vehicle equipped with a fifth wheel, and computing costs from operating costs of the vehicle and the tolls involved. Second, perceived travel times and travel costs were sought through a questionnaire survey, in which origin and destination of the trip, and the route were determined. Data were also collected on socioeconomic variables describing each motorist, the trip purpose, and some attitudinal questions to ascertain if differences were perceived to exist between the toll and free routes.

The modeling technique was based on the use of the logit-form allocation rule from a discriminant analysis.[37] Using the engineering data, a value of $1.82 per hour was determined, while the reported data resulted in a value of $3.82 per hour. It was noted that the engineering data led to a model that misclassified substantially more of the sample than did the reported-data model. The 1967 report[38] concluded with the recommendation that the value of $2.82 be accepted as a working value, since conclusive evidence for adopting either the engineering-based value or the reporting-based value was lacking. It is interesting to note that the researchers reported standard deviations for the value-of-time estimates, which were derived from a coefficient ratio. The reported[39] standard deviation of the value from the reported data was 82 cents per hour and that from the measured data was 40 cents per hour. Since the two time values differed by $2, it was concluded that they were statistically different. However, it has already been noted that the ratio of two normally-distributed variables is not itself normally distributed. Hence, the normal statistical assumptions do not hold and this may be an erroneous conclusion.

In subsequent analyses, investigations were made of the effects of income, amount of time saved, and trip purpose on the value of time.[40] In addition, the Stanford researchers undertook a further analysis of the original data in an effort to determine the reasons for the extent of the difference in the results from the measured and reported data. It is not intended to provide a detailed summary of the results of this work here. The references already noted give a detailed account of the work, together with some dissenting discussion.[41] The results may be summarized briefly in the following manner.

The processes of "adjusting" and "filtering" the data resulted in an increase in the estimated value of time from the measured data to $2.83 with a standard error of 87 cents per hour. At the same time, the processes resulted in a small (probably insignificant) decrease in the reported-data value to $3.78 with a standard error of 92 cents per hour. Further efforts at filtering the data led to a range of reported values of $3.78 to $4.13 per hour, and a range of measured values of $2.83 to $5.78 per hour. The conclusion from this work was that the value from the reported data appeared much more reliable than that from the measured data and the researchers concluded that the probable best constant value of time was about $3.78 per hour.

In the original work, the model used was of the form of equations (4.23) and (4.24).

$$p = \frac{e^{G(X)}}{1 + e^{G(X)}} \tag{4.23}$$

$$G(X) = a_0 + a_1 \Delta t + a_2 \Delta c \tag{4.24}$$

where Δt = time difference

Δc = cost difference

a_0, a_1, a_2 = coefficients derived from revealed behavior

The value of time savings was estimated by means of equation (4.25).

$$V_T = \frac{a_1}{a_2} \tag{4.25}$$

In order to estimate variations in value of time by income, a product term of the form $I \Delta t$ was added to the function of equation (4.24). Thus, the new model is that shown in equation (4.26) and the value of time is given by equation (4.27).

$$G(X) = b_0 + b_1 \Delta t + b_2 \Delta c + b_3 I \; GK;Dt \tag{4.26}$$

$$V_t = \frac{b_1}{b_2} + \frac{b_3 I}{b_2} \tag{4.27}$$

where b_0, b_1, b_2, b_3 = coefficients derived from revealed behavior.

This formulation yields a value of travel time that is a function of income, as desired. It may, however, generate estimation problems resulting from intercorrelations between the terms Δt and $I\Delta t$.

In order to determine variation in the value of travel time by amount of time saved, equation (4.26) was estimated for stratifications of the values of Δt. A number of alternative stratifications were tried for each trip purpose, with the stratification chosen that yielded the statistically best models. In all of this work, the estimates of the coefficients were developed from the adjusted (but not filtered) reported data. The estimation process results in tables of time values by amount of time saved (in three strata), by income group, and by trip purpose. From these results, total benefits are estimated for one-minute increments of time saving. These tables are reported in the 1970 SRI report.[42]

Although this research has sparked some considerable controversy, it remains the largest single effort to measure values of time by conventional methods. It is unfortunate that the researchers failed to perceive the fact that the methodology produced estimated prices of time rather than values of time. Had this fact and its implications been recognized, the research effort might have become the seminal work in value of travel-time savings.

Nevertheless, a number of criticisms must be leveled at this research. The first is, of course, that it has not measured values of time. The second concern is with the reporting of standard errors (or standard deviations) of the values. Since the distribution of a ratio of normally-distributed coefficient values has been shown to be heavily skewed (if it exists at all), the computation of a second moment of the distribution yields little information on the reliability of the ratio. Third, there are a number of other statistical issues that are unresolved. These include the justification for using discriminant analysis,[43] problems of intercorrelation between Δt and $I\Delta t$, and the process of adjusting and filtering data. Fourth, there are parallel conceptual and behavioral issues that are also unresolved. For example, differences in other attributes between the routes were not incorporated in the models, although data were collected on some of these attributes;

the question of whether people can perceive differences in travel times as precisely as by one-minute increments (as implied in the tabulated values) has not been addressed; and the appropriateness of using an interactive income and travel-time difference variable has not been considered from a behavioral viewpoint.[44]

Simultaneously with the research by SRI, a number of other value of time studies were underway both in the United States and the United Kingdom. These studies opened a new generation of estimation of supposed time values (most of them being prices of time) and are the subject of the next section of this chapter.

Some Recent Studies of Time Valuation

The second generation of time-valuation studies can be characterized as being developed from the study of choices of travel mode, rather than choices of route. In some instances, the choice studies had the principal aim of developing time-value estimates, while other studies derived estimates as a secondary product of the development of improved choice models. Again, extensive summaries of these studies are also to be found elsewhere[45] and will not be repeated, though a few highlights of the studies are discussed here.

Almost without exception, the earliest of the studies in this generation were concerned with trips to and from work. Investigations of nonwork, noncommuting travel-time values did not follow until about six years later. Since the studies were performed in several countries, it is easiest to compare results by examining time values as a percentage of the wage rate.

The earliest study of this type was undertaken in Paris in 1962 and used linear regression to formulate a choice model.[46] For two income groups, this study determined a value that was 75% of the wage rate. (In comparison with this, the SRI value of $2.82 was 61% of the wage rate, while the later value of $3.78 was 80%.) Probably the next study, chronologically, was one by Beesley[47] in 1963, which first put forward the concept of trader-analysis by graphical methods. This study yielded time values that ranged from 31 to 49 percent of the wage rate for people choosing between car and public transport.

Subsequently, a number of mode-choice studies were used to develop estimates of time values. The models of mode choice used various curve-fitting techniques, including linear-regression analysis, discriminant, probit, and logit analysis. A wide variation in values is apparent. They range from about 14 percent of the wage rate up to 132 percent. Almost all of the studies referred to here were undertaken between 1964 and 1972. Most of the studies considered only travel times and travel costs as relevant attributes in the choice model, thus not accounting for the circumstances under which the time is spent. Notably, Quarmby[48] split travel time into out-of-vehicle time and in-vehicle time, before estimating an overall value of time of 20-25 percent of the wage rate. Lave[49] took the data used by Lisco[50] and devised a dummy variable for comfort. In so doing he estimated a decrease in the value of travel time from 52 percent to 42 percent of the wage rate.

Among the many other studies undertaken, the principal remaining one that represents a major departure from the other studies discussed here is that of Hensher.[51] This was the pioneering study to attempt to measure the "transfer payment" and to estimate values of time in a trader analysis based upon this value. The technique, which was described earlier in this chapter, resulted in the estimation of time values that ranged between 19 and 27 percent of the wage rate. Estimation, however, did not allow for the effects of other attribute differences, such as comfort and convenience.

One remaining study in this group that should be mentioned is that of Ergün.[52] This was a study of one segment of the commuting trip—the choice of parking location in the downtown area. The study is of particular note because it estimated values from a technique similar to the graphic trader analysis. The technique is named the "indifference-circle method" and attempts to find a minimum misclassification line in a plot of values of time implied by the revealed choice behavior. The value achieved was $4.50 for the sample, which had an average income of over $8,000 per annum. This represents a value for walking time between the parking lot and the workplace. The value is marginally higher than the travel-time values determined by SRI from route choices, but is more nearly a value of time, while the SRI values, as previously noted, are prices of time.

Beginnning in 1967, the United Kingdom Department of the Environment commissioned a number of studies on values of travel time, most of which were set up to estimate values for nonwork, noncommuting trips. In this case, a number of different approaches were taken, including the use of trip-distribution and route-choice models, in addition to the more usual mode-choice models used for commuting trips. Hensher[53] has tabulated the results of these studies through 1971. Since wage rates were not generally reported in the studies, a common metric of percentage of wage rate cannot be used to compare values. Most of the values obtained, however, were in the United Kingdom and are reported in pence per hour. These British values range from 5 pence per hour for in-vehicle time for short trips to libraries to 156 pence per hour for day-trip recreational trips. Even within the group of intercity recreational trips, values were reported from 44 pence per hour to 156 pence per hour. The estimation techniques used were linear, logit, and discriminant analysis and generally did not embody any accounting of other attribute differences. One exception to this was the work of Watson,[54] who devised a proxy variable for convenience, termed a "journey unit." Thus, Watson's values of 43 pence per hour for rail travelers and 53 pence per hour for car travelers can be considered more refined than most of the other values reported.

In summary, beginning with the SRI work in the mid-1960s, there has been a major resurgence of interest and effort in the measurement of values of time for nonworking travel. With very few exceptions, however, the values estimated are average prices of time, not values. In addition, very few of the values have been estimated taking into account the circumstances under which the time is spent.

Concluding Comments

It is pertinent to raise again the question posed at the beginning of this chapter—why are travel-time values needed? It is clearly apparent that few true values of time have been estimated and fewer used in evaluation. Most so-called "values" have, in fact, been shown to be either average or marginal prices of time. It is notable that almost all of the reported studies have taken place in the United States, the United Kingdom, Israel, or Australia. Indeed, the estimation of values of time has been termed the "Anglo-Saxon disease." This fact seems to imply that values of travel time may not be necessary for the evaluation of alternative policies and investments, unless the conclusion is drawn that few other countries undertake such evaluations. Clearly, this latter conclusion is not supported by the evidence.

As has been mentioned earlier in this chapter, the strict application of travel time to evaluation would result in highly inequitable investment and policy decisions from a public welfare viewpoint. Since values of travel time are higher for wealthier people, much higher benefits would be obtained by providing a reserved lane on an expressway for everyone with incomes over, say, $25,000 per annum than by providing a reserved lane for carpools. The fact that such a policy almost certainly would not be given serious consideration does not invalidate the point. Indeed, it might be substantially less far-fetched to suggest that a publicly-owned air line could easily justify providing first-class accommodations only, in order to discriminate against the less wealthy. The benefits of such a policy would, again, be far greater than providing a mix of coach and first class, or all coach class. Of course, profitability is another issue altogether.

Furthermore, if the approach taken by Stanford Research Institute is correct, then the correct use of value of time in evaluation will involve a computation of the amount of time that each facility user will save under any given alternative strategy. It is certain that the techniques to estimate or forecast travel to this degree of detail do not exist at present. It is also unlikely that the techniques ever will exist in the future. Hence, the strict application of time values to the estimation of benefits seems unlikely ever to be feasible.

Strictly within the context of evaluation, it appears that it may be concluded that travel-time values are unlikely to have significant use for many more years. Indeed, in the United States, relatively few evaluations continue to use values of travel time extensively. The practice continues in Britain, Israel, and Australia at present, but may soon begin to decline, as it has in the United States.

On the other hand, time values have considerable utility in the synthesis of travel-forecasting models. Rather than depending upon small-sample data of revealed behavior to determine the appropriate coefficients of travel time and other attributes, the direct use of values of travel time and other attributes can be input in the prior model formulation. The result of this process would be the development of more transferable and more temporally stable travel-forecasting models. Thus, the development of good estimates of travel-time values should result in significant improvements in travel-forecasting capabilities and, concomitantly, improvements in evaluation through more reliable estimates of travel under various potential conditions.

In conclusion, it may be asserted that there is considerable value in the continuation of research into and correct measurement of values of travel time. It is imperative, however, that such measurement be made of the *value* of travel-time savings rather than the *price* of travel-time savings. To date, only those values developed by Hensher,[55] Beesley,[56] Ergün,[57] and Beesley and Stopher[58] can be considered to be *values* of travel time. It seems logical to conclude, furthermore, that the wide diversity in the other measures obtained are due almost entirely to the fact that those measures are *prices* of travel-time savings, which must be expected to vary from one site to another. In contrast, *values* of travel time may be expected to be stable within homogeneous population groups and invariant with location or travel environment.

5 Methods of Evaluation

Introduction

In this chapter four conventional methods for carrying out economic evaluations of transportation facilities are examined. These techniques are annual cost, net present value, benefit cost ratio, and internal rate of return. Each of these techniques constitutes a way of comparing the costs and benefits of alternative proposals, based upon specific interest rates and on specific periods of time for the life of a project. In each case, the formulation used in current engineering practice is investigated. This means that definitions of benefits will generally be according to the highway engineer's definition, but the computation of costs and benefits will be carried out for all individual years instead of for a "representative year." In general, it will also be assumed that capital costs are committed in year 1, and that they are replaced periodically at the end of their service lives.

The notation for the various costs and benefits associated with transportation projects will be the same as that used by Wohl and Martin.[1]

The costs will be:

$CFC_{y,t}$ = capital costs for construction, etc.

$CFO_{y,t}$ = continuing costs of operation and maintenance

$CVC_{y,t}$ = capital costs for vehicles and terminal facilities

$CUT_{y,t}$ = costs for users of travel time (also discomfort and inconvenience, if a monetary equivalent for these is available)

$CVO_{y,t}$ = costs of operation and maintenance for vehicles and terminal facilities

All these costs are for project y in year t. Similarly, in terms of project y and year t, the benefits can be written as:

$BUN_{y,t}$ = nonperceived user benefits

$BUM_{y,t}$ = perceived user benefits

$BOM_{y,t}$ = other nonuser benefits

Using these notations, the mathematical expressions for the four techniques can be developed.

68

Annual Costs

The annual-costs method of evaluation compares alternative proposals on the basis of the average annual costs of each project, over its economic life, and at a given interest rate. These average annual costs are made up of the continuing costs of operation and maintenance, together with the capital costs placed on an equivalent annual basis.

To place capital costs on an equivalent annual basis, they are multiplied by the capital-recovery factor for the designated interest rate and service life of the facility concerned, as is shown in equations (5.1) and (5.2).

$$ECFC_{i,n_F} = (crf_{i,n_F})(CFC_{y,0}) \qquad (5.1)$$

$$ECVC_{i,n_V} = (crf_{i,n_V})(CVC_{y,0}) \qquad (5.2)$$

The remaining costs are continuing costs, and would be calculated for each year. To obtain some of these costs, further calculations are necessary. Although these calculations are common to all the techniques considered in this chapter, they are discussed in detail at this point.

Volume of Travel

It is clear that computations of vehicle operating costs and user travel-time costs will each require information on the volume of travel on the facility in question. The standard practice of highway engineers is to use an average daily traffic figure over the project life. Thus, for instance, if an alternative has a life of 20 years, and traffic is expected to grow at the rate of 300,000 trips per year from an initial volume of 13.5 million trips per year, the highway engineer would compute the average annual volume as follows:

$$\text{Average annual volume} = 13.5 + 10 \times 0.3 \text{ million trips}$$

$$= 16.5 \text{ million trips}$$

If user costs were, say, $0.65 per mile per vehicle, and the facility was 20 miles in length, average annual users costs would be:

$$\text{Average annual user costs} = \$0.65 \times 20 \times 16.5 \text{ million}$$

$$= \$214.5 \text{ million}$$

This method tends to overstate user costs in several ways. First, no account is taken of a discounting of future user costs as the project life is approached. Second, a steady growth rate is assumed to take place, and no allowance is made for a rapid initial growth, followed by a gradual decrease in the growth rate.

An alternative formulation that has been suggested is the use of an equivalent annual traffic volume, given by equation (5.3).

$$EATV_{i,n} = a + \frac{g}{i} - \frac{ng}{i}(crf_{i,n} - i) \qquad (5.3)$$

where a = the initial annual travel volume

g = the growth rate

Assuming a linear traffic growth, and $i = 6\%$, with $n = 20$ years, $crf_{i,n} = 0.08718$. The appropriate computation is shown in equation (5.4).

$$EATV_{i,n} = 13.5 \text{ million} + \frac{0.3 \text{ million}}{0.06}$$

$$- \frac{20 \times 0.3 \text{ million}}{0.06}(0.08718 - 0.6)$$

$$= 15.782 \text{ million trips} \qquad (5.4)$$

Clearly, the equivalent annual user costs will be less than the average annual user costs. In this example, equivalent annual user costs will be $205.166 millions, which is less by nearly $10 millions (or 5%). The longer the period of time, and the higher the interest rate, the greater will be the discrepancy between these figures. Even this method, however, assumes a constant growth rate and also assumes a constant user cost per mile.

More correctly, the analysis should be carried out on a detailed year-by-year basis. In this case, the annual traffic volume is computed for each year. Since the volume determines the speed of travel, and consequently the user costs, speed and user cost information must also be computed for each year, based on the expected travel volume. Future user costs must then be discounted by using the present worth factor $pwf_{i,t}$ appropriate for the year and interest rate, and may then be summed to yield the total present value of user costs.

In chapter 2 the fact was discussed that travel volumes vary throughout the day, and that a particular price-volume curve and a particular demand curve refer to a specific facility at a specific time and to one individual user. Implicitly, the variations of traffic volume over the design period represent a plot of the changes in location of the equilibrium between supply and demand. Thus, some simplifications of this situation have to be made to avoid having to perform a very large number of calculations of price and volume. The principle simplifications introduced are to assume an "average demand curve" and to use an "average price-volume curve" with calculations of price and volume under average peak and average off-peak conditions. Thus, it will be assumed that through the peak period, the travel volume remains constant and then drops to a new, lower constant value during the off-peak.

It is suggested by Wohl and Martin[2] that the price-volume curve may be represented mathematically by equation (5.5).

$$p = b + \frac{f}{v_0 - aq} \qquad (5.5)$$

where b, f, a = constants for a facility

v_0 = "free-flow" speed

q = the volume

p = price

Assumptions must then be made about the volumes of travel in the peak and off-peak as a function of total average daily traffic on the facility. These assumptions will yield values q_p and q_o for peak and off-peak, respectively, which will enable a calculation to be made of the prices p_p and p_o. Thus, estimates may be made of the user prices for each year of the service life of the facility.

Other Costs and Benefits

Calculations of the volume and user price of travel on the facility lead to ready calculation of most of the other costs and benefits. Capital costs of the facility are relatively straightforward. The major problem that still remains concerns the calculations of user benefits and user travel costs.[3]

Using an approach in which consumer surplus is included, the total travel benefit is equal to the price of travel times the volume of use on the facility, i.e., $p_p q_p$ and $p_o q_o$ for peak and off-peak, respectively. User taxes will represent a part of the user travel price as perceived by the traveler. However, as was mentioned before, user taxes that contribute to the payment for the facility must not be included in user costs *in addition to* capital and maintenance costs. The reason for this, it must be stressed, is not because such taxes are not part of user travel price, but is because the inclusion of user taxes, and capital and maintenance costs, would lead to double counting of costs. Hence, user travel costs will be equal to the perceived travel price *minus* user taxes. If the user travel price obtained from the earlier analysis is a true measure of perceived travel price, then the user travel costs will be the user travel benefit minus user taxes. This is, in fact, a somewhat extensive simplification, principally because the price of travel determined from equilibrium considerations of price-volume and demand curves will not be the total travel costs, but only perceived travel cost. Thus, the analysis should ideally constitute several important parts.

First, the perceived price of travel can be computed from demand and price-volume equilibrium. Analysis is then needed to determine total real costs of time, inconvenience, discomfort, and vehicle operation and maintenance. The latter costs represent the total perceived and nonperceived user costs. From these costs, user taxes should be deducted and the balance multiplied by the volume of use on the facility for the computed perceived travel price. This will yield total user travel cost.

Annual-Cost Calculations

Considerations of the computation of annual costs for a proposed facility can now be continued. The annual costs method simply requires the computation of total annual costs in a representative year for the facility, and the decision would be in favor of the least annual cost proposal. Equation (5.6), which is the typical highway engineer's definition using a representative year, expresses this method mathematically.

$$[TAC_{y,\bar{n}}]_i = ECFC_{y,i,n_F} + ECVC_{y,i,n_v} + CFO_{y,\bar{n}}$$

$$+ CUT_{y,\bar{n}} + CVO_{y,\bar{n}} \tag{5.6}$$

Alternatively, the correct discounted total annual costs, using a stream of costs over the life of the project, is shown in equation (5.7).

$$[DTAC_{y,n}]_i = ECFC_{y,i,n_F} + ECVC_{y,i,n_v}$$

$$+ \sum_t (pwf_{i,t})\,(CFO_{y,t} + CUT_{y,t} + CVO_{y,t}) \tag{5.7}$$

Implicitly, this method assumes that the benefits from all the alternatives are the same, since the benefits are not included. Clearly, the alternative of abandonment of the facility cannot be considered since this would always be the recommended plan because it has no costs associated with it.

Since, in general, the travel volumes, travel prices, and hence travel benefits, will rarely be the same, the method is unlikely to give correct results in terms of a comparison of the costs and benefits of each alternative. Also, because of the point just noted concerning facility abandonment, the method will tend to yield seriously suboptimal results. It is therefore not to be recommended as an evaluation method. Nevertheless, the results of the application of this method should be noted in the context of a comparison with other methods.

In order better to understand the implications and results of this and subsequently discussed methods, it is desirable to examine an example which is used to demonstrate the required calculations.

Example

A specific transportation problem is considered within the mythical West Cupcake Area Transportation Study (WECATS). Within a specific transportation corridor, four alternatives have been proposed. Alternative 0 is the do-nothing alternative. Alternative 1 comprises the upgrading of two arterial highways by widening, traffic signals, improved intersection designs, and the introduction of a median. Posted speed limits would be raised by these means, and traffic signals linked for posted speed. Alternative 2 calls for more extensive upgrading by building grade-separated interchanges at the six major intersections and traffic signals at the others. In addition, the other changes of Alternative 1 will also be incorporated. Alternative 3 calls for no change in either of the arterials, but the addition of a parallel urban freeway.

It is assumed that the traffic growth has been determined by analysis of the equilibrium of price-volume and demand relationships and that, for each facility, there is an approximately linear growth of traffic over the twenty-year planning horizon. These growth rates are shown in Figure 5-1, and are represented by equations (5.8) through (5.11).

$$AV_{0,t} = 13.5 + 0.30t \qquad (5.8)$$

$$AV_{1,t} = 16.0 + 0.50t \qquad (5.9)$$

$$AV_{2,t} = 18.3 + 0.555t \qquad (5.10)$$

$$AV_{3,t} = 21.0 + 0.6875t \qquad (5.11)$$

These annual volumes $AV_{y,t}$ are in millions of trips. The annual volumes for each year are given in Table 5-1. It is assumed that each day comprises 4 hours of peak traffic and 14 hours of off-peak traffic. It is further assumed that 40% of Annual Average Daily Traffic (AADT) will occur in peak hours, resulting in 10% of AADT per peak hour. Furthermore, it is assumed that there are 20 hours of peak traffic per week and 106 hours of off-peak traffic. Thus, the annual volume of travel comprises approximately 1,040 hours of peak travel and 5,512 hours of off-peak travel. It will be assumed that the peak continues to contain the same proportion of AADT throughout the analysis period (this is not likely to be realistic, but simplifies the computations). The hourly peak and off-peak flows are given in Tables 5-2 and 5-3.

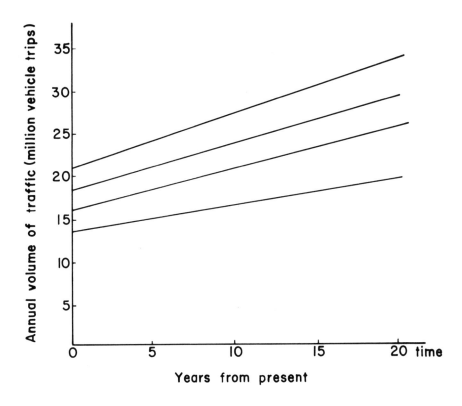

Figure 5-1. Growth Rates for Evaluation Example.

These flows were calculated from the volumes in Table 5-1 using equations (5.12) and (5.13).

$$q_p = \frac{AV}{3640} \tag{5.12}$$

$$q_o = \frac{AV - 1040q_p}{5512} \tag{5.13}$$

At this point, the volumes of travel on the proposed alternative facilities are known. Now the total price of travel on each facility needs to be determined, together with the user travel cost for the computation of operation, maintenance, and time costs for the users. Equation (5.14) represents an assumed price-volume relationship.

$$p = b + \frac{f}{v_0 - aq} \quad \text{cents/trip mile} \tag{5.14}$$

Table 5-1
Annual Travel Volume for Each Project in Millions of Trips

	Project			
Year	*0*	*1*	*2*	*3*
1	13.8	16.5	18.85	21.68
2	14.1	17.0	19.41	22.37
3	14.4	17.5	19.96	23.06
4	14.7	18.0	20.52	23.75
5	15.0	18.5	21.07	24.43
6	15.3	19.0	21.63	25.12
7	15.6	19.5	22.18	25.81
8	15.9	20.0	22.74	26.50
9	16.2	20.5	23.29	27.18
10	16.5	21.0	23.85	27.87
11	16.8	21.5	24.40	28.56
12	17.1	22.0	24.96	29.25
13	17.4	22.5	25.51	29.93
14	17.7	23.0	26.07	30.62
15	18.0	23.5	26.62	31.31
16	18.3	24.0	27.18	32.00
17	18.6	24.5	27.73	32.68
18	18.9	25.0	28.29	33.37
19	19.2	25.5	28.84	34.06
20	19.5	26.0	29.4	34.75

Table 5-2
Peak Hourly Flows for Each Project (Vehicle Trips)

	Project			
Year	*0*	*1*	*2*	*3*
1	3791	4532	5179	5958
2	3873	4670	5332	6146
3	3956	4807	5484	6335
4	4038	4945	5637	6524
5	4120	5082	5789	6713
6	4203	5219	5942	6902
7	4285	5357	6094	7091
8	4368	5494	6247	7280
9	4450	5631	6399	7469
10	4532	5769	6552	7657
11	4615	5906	6704	7846
12	4697	6043	6857	8035
13	4780	6181	7009	8224
14	4862	6318	7162	8413
15	4945	6456	7314	8602
16	5027	6593	7467	8791
17	5109	6730	7619	8980
18	5192	6868	7771	9168
19	5274	7005	7924	9357
20	5357	7142	8076	9546

Table 5-3
Off-Peak Hourly Flows for Each Project (Vehicle Trips)

Year	Project 0	1	2	3
1	1788	2138	2443	2810
2	1827	2202	2515	2899
3	1866	2267	2587	2988
4	1904	2332	2659	3077
5	1943	2397	2731	3166
6	1982	2462	2802	3255
7	2021	2526	2874	3344
8	2060	2591	2946	3434
9	2099	2656	3018	3523
10	2138	2721	3090	3612
11	2177	2786	3162	3701
12	2215	2850	3234	3790
13	2254	2915	3306	3879
14	2293	2980	3378	3968
15	2332	3045	3450	4057
16	2371	3110	3522	4146
17	2410	3174	3594	4235
18	2449	3239	3666	4324
19	2488	3304	3737	4414
20	2526	3369	3809	4503

The price of travel for the four alternatives is shown in equations (5.15) through (5.18).

$$\text{Alternative 0:} \quad p = 7.0 + \frac{350}{25 - 0.003q} \qquad (5.15)$$

$$\text{Alternative 1:} \quad p = 6.0 + \frac{350}{42 - 0.004q} \qquad (5.16)$$

$$\text{Alternative 2:} \quad p = 6.0 + \frac{350}{47 - 0.004q} \qquad (5.17)$$

$$\text{Alternative 3:} \quad p = 6.0 + \frac{350}{66 - 0.005q} \qquad (5.18)$$

where q is the hourly volume. The complexity of these expressions makes it easier to compute travel speeds ($= v_0 - aq$) first. These are given in Table 5-4. Then, the total benefit (equal to user cost multiplied by volume) can be computed. First, the user price of travel, or user benefit is computed, as shown in Table 5-5. Using Tables 5-2 and 5-3, the total hourly benefits can be calculated, as shown in Table 5-6. For the computations required, the benefits have to be accrued as total annual benefits. This can

Table 5-4
Average Peak and Off-Peak Speeds (mph)

	Project							
	0		1		2		3	
Year	Peak	Off-Peak	Peak	Off-Peak	Peak	Off-Peak	Peak	Off-Peak
1	13.6	19.6	23.8	33.4	26.2	37.2	36.2	51.9
2	13.3	19.5	23.3	33.1	25.6	36.9	35.2	51.5
3	13.1	19.4	22.7	32.9	25.0	36.6	34.3	51.0
4	12.8	19.2	22.2	32.6	24.4	26.3	33.3	50.6
5	12.6	19.1	21.6	32.4	23.8	36.0	32.4	50.1
6	12.3	19.0	21.1	32.1	23.2	35.7	31.4	49.7
7	12.1	18.9	20.5	31.8	22.6	35.5	30.5	49.2
8	11.8	18.8	20.0	31.6	22.0	35.2	29.5	48.8
9	11.6	18.7	19.4	31.3	21.4	34.9	28.6	48.3
10	11.4	18.5	18.9	31.1	20.7	34.6	27.7	47.9
11	11.1	18.4	18.3	30.8	20.1	34.3	26.7	47.4
12	10.9	18.3	17.8	30.5	19.5	34.0	25.8	47.0
13	10.6	18.2	17.2	30.3	18.9	33.7	24.8	46.6
14	10.4	18.1	16.7	30.0	18.3	33.4	23.9	46.1
15	10.1	18.0	16.1	29.8	17.7	33.1	22.9	45.7
16	9.9	17.8	15.6	29.5	17.1	32.9	22.0	45.2
17	9.6	17.7	15.0	29.3	16.5	32.6	21.0	44.8
18	9.4	17.6	14.5	29.0	15.9	32.3	20.1	44.3
19	9.1	17.5	13.9	28.7	15.3	32.0	19.2	43.9
20	8.9	17.4	13.4	28.5	14.6	31.7	18.2	43.4

be done by multiplying the peak hourly benefit by 1040, and the off-peak hourly benefits by 5512, as given in Table 5-7. Thus, these total user travel benefits are computed as shown in equation (5.19).

$$TAUB = 1040\ PHB + 5512\ OHB \qquad (5.19)$$

where PHB and OHB are, respectively, the peak hourly benefits and the off-peak hourly benefits, as shown in Table 5-6. For use in the process of evaluation the annual benefits need to be discounted at some interest rate. For this, each annual benefit must be multiplied by its relevant present-worth factor.

As a part of the examination of evaluation methods, three different interest rates are used: 5%, 8%, and 10%. This illustrates the effect of interest rates on the different techniques. The discounted annual benefits are given in Table 5-8, together with total benefits. (Year 0 is omitted, since only the existing highway would exist in year 0.)

In order to arrive at the user costs, the user taxes need to be deducted (based on the simplifying assumption made earlier). To further simplify

Table 5-5
Total User Benefit in Cents/Trip-Mile

	Project							
	0		1		2		3	
Year	Peak	Off-Peak	Peak	Off-Peak	Peak	Off-Peak	Peak	Off-Peak
1	32.6	24.8	20.6	16.4	19.3	15.4	15.6	12.7
2	33.1	24.9	21.0	16.5	19.6	15.4	15.9	12.7
3	33.6	25.0	21.3	16.6	19.9	15.5	16.1	12.8
4	34.1	25.1	21.7	16.7	20.3	15.6	16.4	12.9
5	34.6	25.2	22.1	16.7	20.6	15.7	16.7	12.9
6	35.2	25.3	22.5	16.8	21.0	15.7	17.1	13.0
7	35.8	25.4	23.0	16.9	21.4	15.8	17.4	13.1
8	36.4	25.5	23.4	17.0	21.9	15.9	17.8	13.1
9	37.0	25.7	23.9	17.1	22.3	16.0	18.2	13.2
10	37.6	25.8	24.4	17.2	22.8	16.1	18.6	13.3
11	38.3	25.9	25.0	17.3	23.3	16.1	19.0	13.3
12	39.0	26.0	25.6	17.4	23.8	16.2	19.5	13.4
13	39.8	26.1	26.2	17.5	24.4	16.3	20.0	13.5
14	40.6	26.3	26.9	17.6	25.0	16.4	20.6	13.5
15	41.4	26.4	27.6	17.7	25.7	16.5	21.2	13.6
16	42.2	26.5	28.3	17.8	26.4	16.6	21.8	13.7
17	43.1	26.6	29.2	17.9	27.1	16.7	22.5	13.8
18	44.1	26.8	30.0	18.0	27.9	16.8	23.2	13.8
19	45.1	26.9	31.0	18.1	28.8	16.9	24.2	13.9
20	46.2	27.0	32.0	18.2	29.8	17.0	25.1	14.0

matters, the same tax rates and manner of application as in Wohl and Martin[4] is assumed. Thus, *UFM* is 0.2859 cents/vehicle-mile and *UVM* is 9.915 cents/gallon of gas. The weighted average speeds over the total planning period need to be computed for each facility proposal. These weighted average speeds are given in Table 5-9. Total user taxes can then be determined by applying these taxes per vehicle mile to the volume data in Table 5-1. These taxes must be discounted before being subtracted from the user benefits of Table 5-8. The simplest, but most tedious, way of doing this is to discount each year's taxes, and sum the total. This may be represented mathematically as shown in equation (5.20).

$$TAT = \frac{AT_1}{1 + i} + \frac{AT_2}{(1 + i)^2} + \frac{AT_3}{(1 + i)^3} + \ldots + \frac{AT_n}{(1 + i)^n} \qquad (5.20)$$

However, since user taxes are proportional to volume, it may be noted that $AT_p = (UT)(AV_p)$, and the annual volume AV_p increases linearly, in this example, by a growth factor g. Hence, the expression for *TAT* may be rewritten as in equations (5.21) and (5.22).

78

Table 5-6
Total Hourly User Benefits in Dollars/Trip-Mile

	Project							
	0		1		2		3	
Year	Peak	Off-Peak	Peak	Off-Peak	Peak	Off-Peak	Peak	Off-Peak
1	1239	443	936	352	1000	376	933	357
2	1284	455	981	364	1046	389	978	371
3	1331	467	1027	377	1095	402	1026	384
4	1379	479	1075	389	1145	415	1075	397
5	1429	490	1125	402	1197	428	1127	410
6	1481	503	1178	415	1251	442	1181	424
7	1535	515	1232	428	1308	455	1238	438
8	1590	527	1290	442	1368	469	1297	452
9	1648	539	1350	455	1430	483	1360	466
10	1708	552	1413	469	1496	497	1426	480
11	1771	564	1479	483	1565	512	1496	494
12	1836	577	1549	497	1637	526	1571	509
13	1904	590	1623	511	1714	541	1650	524
14	1974	603	1701	525	1795	555	1735	539
15	2048	616	1784	540	1881	570	1825	554
16	2126	630	1872	554	1973	585	1923	569
17	2207	643	1966	569	2071	601	2028	584
18	2292	657	2066	584	2175	616	2142	600
19	2381	670	2174	600	2287	632	2266	616
20	2475	684	2290	615	2408	648	2402	632

$$TAT = \frac{AT_1}{(1+i)} + \frac{AT_1 + g}{(1+i)^2} + \frac{AT_1 + 2g}{(1+i)^3} + \ldots$$

$$+ \frac{AT_1 + (n-1)g}{(1+i)^n} \tag{5.21}$$

$$TAT = (AT_1)pwf_{i,n} + g \sum_{p=1}^{n} \frac{(p-1)}{(1+i)^p} \tag{5.22}$$

It can be shown that the second term of equation (5.22) may be written as in equations (5.23) and (5.24).

$$g\sum\frac{(p-1)}{(1+i)^p} = g\left[\frac{(1+i)^n - 1}{i^2(1+i)^n} - \frac{n}{i(1+i)^n}\right] \tag{5.23}$$

$$g\sum\frac{(p-1)}{(1+i)^p} = \frac{g}{i}[pwf_{i,n} - n\,pwf'_{i,n}] \tag{5.24}$$

where $pwf'_{i,n}$ is the present worth factor for year n, as distinguished from $pwf_{i,n}$ which is the sum of pwfs for n years from the present.

Table 5-7
Total Annual User Benefits for each Project
(In Thousands of Dollars)

	Project			
Year	*0*	*1*	*2*	*3*
1	3735	2914	3114	2943
2	3846	3029	3234	3063
3	3960	3147	3356	3184
4	4075	3267	3481	3309
5	4193	3390	3608	3437
6	4313	3516	3739	3568
7	4436	3646	3874	3703
8	4561	3779	4011	3842
9	4690	3916	4153	3984
10	4821	4057	4299	4132
11	4956	4202	4449	4284
12	5094	4351	4604	4442
13	5235	4506	4765	4605
14	5381	4666	4931	4775
15	5530	4833	5103	4953
16	5684	5005	5281	5138
17	5842	5185	5468	5333
18	6005	5372	5662	5538
19	6173	5569	5865	5755
20	6347	5775	6079	5985

Thus, for instance, project 0, at 5%, will have total discounted annual taxes according to the computations shown in equations (5.25) through (5.27). All annual taxes are shown in Table 5-10.

$$TAT = \left\{(13.8)\frac{1}{0.08024} + \frac{0.30}{0.05}\left[\frac{1}{0.08024} - (20)0.3769\right]\right\}0.881 \quad (5.25)$$

$$TAT = \{172.0 + 6\,[14.48 - 7.538]\}0.881 \text{ ten thousand dollars}$$
$$\text{per mile} \quad (5.26)$$

$$TAT = \$1,775,000 \text{ per mile} \quad (5.27)$$

At this point, user costs, including travel time, vehicle operation, and vehicle maintenance have been computed. Total user benefits have also been determined where users are defined as users of the new facility proposed, and do not include users of other parts of the network, who may have received benefits from the new facility. In this example, nonuser benefits are also excluded. The remaining data required are those of capital and continuing costs of the facility, appropriately discounted.

The capital costs are assumed to take place at year 0, and right-of-way is assumed to have an indefinite life. It is assumed that construction costs

Table 5-8
Discounted Total Annual Benefits for Each Project
(In Thousands of Dollars per Mile)

Year	Project 0			Project 1			Project 2			Project 3		
	5%	*8%*	*10%*	*5%*	*8%*	*10%*	*5%*	*8%*	*10%*	*5%*	*8%*	*10%*
1	3,577	3,459	3,396	2,775	2,698	2,649	2,966	2,884	2,831	2,803	2,725	2,676
2	3,489	3,298	3,179	2,747	2,597	2,503	2,933	2,772	2,673	2,778	2,626	2,531
3	3,420	3,143	2,975	2,718	2,498	2,364	2,899	2,664	2,521	2,751	2,528	2,392
4	3,352	2,995	2,783	2,688	2,401	2,231	2,863	2,558	2,377	2,772	2,432	2,260
5	3,285	2,853	2,603	2,656	2,307	2,105	2,827	2,456	2,240	2,693	2,339	2,134
6	3,218	2,718	2,434	2,624	2,216	1,985	2,790	2,356	2,111	2,663	2,248	2,014
7	3,152	2,588	2,276	2,591	2,127	1,871	2,753	2,260	1,988	2,631	2,160	1,900
8	3,087	2,464	2,128	2,558	2,041	1,763	2,715	2,167	1,871	2,600	2,075	1,792
9	3,023	2,346	1,989	2,524	1,959	1,660	2,677	2,077	1,761	2,568	1,993	1,689
10	2,960	2,233	1,858	2,490	1,879	1,564	2,639	1,991	1,657	2,536	1,913	1,593
11	2,897	2,125	1,737	2,456	1,802	1,472	2,601	1,908	1,559	2,504	1,837	1,501
12	2,836	2,023	1,623	2,423	1,728	1,386	2,564	1,828	1,467	2,473	1,763	1,415
13	2,776	1,925	1,516	2,389	1,657	1,305	2,527	1,752	1,380	2,442	1,693	1,334
14	2,717	1,832	1,417	2,357	1,588	1,228	2,490	1,678	1,298	2,412	1,625	1,257
15	2,660	1,743	1,323	2,324	1,523	1,156	2,454	1,608	1,221	2,382	1,561	1,185
16	2,603	1,659	1,237	2,293	1,461	1,089	2,419	1,541	1,149	2,354	1,500	1,118
17	2,548	1,578	1,155	2,262	1,401	1,025	2,385	1,477	1,081	2,327	1,441	1,055
18	2,495	1,502	1,080	2,232	1,344	966	2,352	1,417	1,018	2,301	1,386	996
19	2,443	1,430	1,009	2,203	1,290	910	2,321	1,359	959	2,277	1,333	941
20	2,392	1,361	943	2,176	1,239	858	2,291	1,304	903	2,255	1,284	889
Total	58,922	45,284	38,670	49,497	37,765	32,101	52,477	40,068	34,075	50,482	38,473	32,681

Table 5-9
Computations of User Taxes

Project	Weighted Average Speed (mph)	Gasoline Consumption (gal/veh.-mile)	User Taxes (cents/vehicle-mile)		
			Variable Component	Fixed Component	Total
0	13.5	0.060	0.595	0.286	0.881
1	22.5	0.050	0.496	0.286	0.782
2	25.1	0.052	0.516	0.286	0.802
3	34.5	0.070	0.694	0.286	0.980

Table 5-10
Total Discounted User Taxes over 20 Years
per Mile of Facility
(In Thousands of Dollars)

Project	5%	8%	10%
0	1775	1376	1182
1	1993	1536	1315
2	2322	1792	1534
3	3312	2552	2183

Table 5-11
Facility Costs per Mile for Each Project

Project	Initial Capital Outlays		Annual Maintenance & Operation
	Construction	Right-of-Way	
0	0	0	$47,500
1	$ 450,000	0	$32,600
2	$ 800,000	0	$29,500
3	$1,125,000	$460,000	$27,300

must be replaced at 20 years. The basic facility costs are as given in Table 5-11. These are discounted, and total discounted costs are given in Tables 5-12 and 5-13. In totaling the costs of the facility, the salvage value of the right-of-way (since this has an indefinite life) has to be considered. The salvage value, which is the present value of the price for which the right-of-way can be sold in 20 years' time, has to be deducted from the costs.

Table 5-12
Discounted Construction and Right-of-Way Costs

Project	5%	8%	10%
0			
Construction	—	—	—
Right-of-Way	—	—	—
Right-of-Way Salvage	—	—	—
1			
Construction	450	450	450
Right-of-Way	—	—	—
Right-of-Way Salvage	—	—	—
2			
Construction	800	800	800
Right-of-Way	—	—	—
Right-of-Way Salvage	—	—	—
3			
Construction	1125	1125	1125
Right-of-Way	460	460	460
Right-of-Way Salvage	−173	−99	−68

Table 5-13
Accumulated and Discounted Continuing Costs

Project	5%	8%	10%
0	592	466	404
1	406	320	278
2	368	290	251
3	340	268	232

This amount is shown in Table 5-12. Finally, the continuing costs of the facility have to be accumulated and discounted, and these are given in Table 5-13. This completes the basic information needed for an example of the application of each of these methods.

All costs associated with the project have been reduced by discounting. For the annual-costs method, the discounted costs are summed and multiplied by the appropriate capital-recovery factor. The details of this are given in Table 5-14. From Table 5-14, it can be seen that the annual-cost method favors a decision for project 1 in each case. The decision here appears to be largely independent of the interest rate. Since the benefits

Table 5-14
Annual-Costs Method—Summary of Calculations

Costs	5%				8%				10%			
	0	1	2	3	0	1	2	3	0	1	2	3
Construction	0	450	800	1,125	0	450	800	1,125	0	450	800	1,125
Right-of-Way	0	0	0	287	0	0	0	361	0	0	0	392
Maintenance	592	406	368	340	466	320	290	268	404	278	251	232
User	57,147	47,504	50,155	47,170	43,908	36,229	38,276	35,921	37,488	30,786	32,541	30,498
Total Discounted Costs	57,739	48,360	51,323	48,922	44,374	36,999	39,366	37,675	37,892	31,514	33,592	32,247
Annual Cost	4,633	3,881	4,118	3,926	4,520	3,768	4,009	3,837	4,451	3,702	3,946	3,788

Table 5-15
Annual Trips, User Benefits, and User Taxes for the Tenth Year

Project	Annual Trips (millions)	Annual User Benefits ($1,000s)	Annual User Taxes ($1,000s)
0	16.5	4956	145
1	21.0	4202	164
2	23.85	4449	192
3	27.88	4284	273

for each project are not identical, it is clear that the annual-cost method will yield incorrect information for decision making.

It should be noted that the analysis just performed was carried out, as far as possible, using strict economic procedures. The standard highway engineering solution would have been different. The highway engineer would have used average user costs and average maintenance costs for the purposes of analysis. The average annual volumes on the facilities occur in the tenth year (since growth is uniform and linear). The tenth year is, therefore, designated as year $\bar{n}$, and the computations are carried out for that year. Total annual vehicle trips, annual user benefits, and annual user taxes are given in Table 5-15. Even here, the analysis is more strictly correct than the average highway engineering analysis, since an average user price would probably have been used. Using this set of figures, the analysis would appear as shown in Table 5-16.

The decision is again the same, but the annual costs are different, and are in different proportion to each other. It is, therefore, clear that this identical outcome could not have been guaranteed, and is largely fortuitous with this set of data.

Net Present Worth Method

The net present worth method comprises simply the determination of the present value, or present worth, of the total benefits less the total costs.[5] The computation of the net present worth for a representative year is given by equation (5.28).

$$[NPV_{y,\bar{n}}]_i = BUN_{y,\bar{n}} + BUM_{y,\bar{n}} + BOM_{y,\bar{n}} - CFC_{y,i,n_F} - CFO_{y,\bar{n}}$$

$$- CVC_{y,i,n_v} - CVO_{y,\bar{n}} - CUT_{y,\bar{n}} \tag{5.28}$$

Table 5-16
Annual-Costs Method—Calculations for Tenth (Representative) Year

Costs	5%				8%				10%			
	0	1	2	3	0	1	2	3	0	1	2	3
Construction	0	450	800	1125	0	450	800	1125	0	450	800	1125
Right-of-Way	0	0	0	287	0	0	0	361	0	0	0	392
Equivalent Capital	0	36.1	64.1	113.2	0	45.8	81.4	151.2	0	52.9	94.0	178.1
Maintenance	47.5	32.6	29.5	27.3	47.5	32.6	29.5	27.3	47.5	32.6	29.5	27.3
User Costs	4811	4078	4257	4011	4811	4078	4257	4011	4811	4078	4257	4011
Total Annual Costs	4858.5	4596.7	5150.6	5563.5	4858.5	4606.4	5167.8	5675.5	4858.5	4613.5	5180.5	5733.4
Decision		√				√				√		

Alternatively, the net present worth can be computed as shown in equation (5.29), using a stream of discounted benefits and costs over the life of the project.

$$NPV_i = \sum_{t=0}^{n}(pwf_{i,t})(BUN_{y,t} + BUM_{y,t} + BOM_{y,t}) - \sum_{t=0}^{n}(pwf_{i,t})$$

$$\times (CFC_{y,t} + CFO_{y,t} + CVC_{y,t} + CVO_{y,t} + CUT_{y,t}) \quad (5.29)$$

where n = the planning horizon

i = the discount rate

Any project with a net present value less than zero is automatically rejected. The project chosen is that one that yields the highest net present value. In the event that benefits are identical, the net present worth method is identical to the annual-cost method, except that the latter cannot permit a decision on abandonment. Clearly, the net present worth method can be used to determine whether or not abandonment is economically feasible.

In deriving the various tables of costs and benefits, all costs and benefits were already discounted by the interest rates studied in this example. Therefore, the analysis for this method may be readily accomplished. Values for this analysis are presented in Table 5-17.

In this case a decision is made in favor of project 3 at 5% and project 0 at 8% and 10%, in contrast to the decision from annual costs, which favored project 1 at all interest rates. It should be noted that the order of preference in the projects changes as the interest rate changes. At 5%, the order is 3, 0, 2, 1; at 8% it is 0, 3, 1, 2; and at 10% it is 0, 1, 2, 3. Clearly, then, the present worth method is sensitive to the interest rate, and as the interest rate becomes higher, will probably favor the low initial-cost alternatives.

The Benefit/Cost Ratio

The benefit/cost ratio method, or cost-benefit method, represents a means whereby a series of projects can be compared by examining successive pairs of projects.[6] Simply, the benefit/cost ratio is defined as

$$B/C = \frac{\text{Increment of benefits between 2 alternatives}}{\text{Increment of highway costs between 2 alternatives}}$$

Costs and benefits are each computed as total discounted costs and benefits for the planning period. Hence, the discount rate must again be determined for the analysis to proceed. Since the discount rate will usually be

Table 5-17
Analysis for Net Present Worth (Value) Method

Costs	5%				8%				10%			
	0	1	2	3	0	1	2	3	0	1	2	3
Construction	0	450	800	1,125	0	450	800	1,125	0	450	800	1,125
Right-of-Way	0	0	0	287	0	0	0	361	0	0	0	392
Maintenance	592	406	368	340	466	320	290	268	404	278	251	232
User Travel Costs	57,147	47,504	50,155	47,170	43,908	36,229	38,276	35,921	37,488	30,786	32,541	30,498
Total Discounted Costs	57,739	48,360	51,323	48,922	44,374	36,999	39,366	37,675	37,892	31,514	33,592	32,247
Total Discounted Benefits	58,922	45,284	38,670	49,497	37,765	32,101	52,477	40,068	34,075	50,482	38,473	32,681
Net Present Value	1,183	1,137	1,155	1,560	910	767	703	798	777	588	483	434

set as the minimum attractive return on the capital involved, any alternative that has a benefit/cost ratio less than one (1.0) is automatically rejected. (This would be analagous to rejecting out-of-hand any alternative that gave a negative net present worth.)

In computing benefit/cost ratios, it is important to compare the high-cost to the low-cost alternative. The ratio is computed as the increment of benefits divided by the increment of costs, and the increment of costs must *always* be positive. The necessity for this can be illustrated by a simple example:

Two alternatives, A and B, have the following characteristics:

	Annual Cost	Annual Benefit	B/C
A	2,000	3,000	1.5
B	3,000	5,000	1.67

Then, if alternative B is compared to alternative A, the results of equation (5.30) develop.

$$B/C = \frac{5,000 - 3,000}{3,000 - 2,000} = \frac{2,000}{1,000} = 2.0 \qquad (5.30)$$

Therefore, alternative B is chosen since the benefit/cost ratio is greater than unity. This is also logical based on a comparison of the individual B/C ratios of the two alternatives. However, if A had been compared to B, equation (5.31) would have resulted.

$$B/C = \frac{3,000 - 5,000}{2,000 - 3,000} = \frac{-2,000}{-1,000} = +2.0 \qquad (5.31)$$

This would clearly suggest that A should be selected. Hence, the procedure must always be to compare the higher-cost alternative to the lower-cost alternative.

The procedure is to compute the benefit/cost ratio for each project first. All projects that yield a benefit cost ratio greater than 1.0 are economically feasible since they will produce economic returns that are at least as great as the discount rate. To determine the *best* alternative requires the computation of incremental benefit/cost ratios. This procedure is performed by arranging alternatives in order of increasing costs. Then, the second lowest cost alternative is compared to the lowest cost alternative, and so forth up to the highest cost. The project is selected that has the highest cost, and both overall and incremental benefit/cost ratios greater than unity.

With a large number of alternatives, the number of comparisons, or incremental benefit/cost ratios, to be computed would become excessively large. It becomes desirable, therefore, to reduce the number of comparisons. In comparing a series of alternatives 1, 2, ... k, if there is an alternative i for which equation (5.32) holds, where alternative i has higher annual costs than alternative j, then alternative j can be eliminated, and subsequent alternatives need not be compared with j.

$$B/C_{(i,j)} > 1 \qquad (5.32)$$

Also, if under the same conditions equation (5.33) holds, then alternative i can be eliminated from all further comparisons.

$$B/C_{(i,j)} < 1 \qquad (5.33)$$

In general terms, if any alternative i is found to be superior to another, j, comparison of the remaining higher cost alternatives to j is unnecessary.

Given this information, the benefit/cost ratio method may be applied to the sample problem. Using data from Table 5-17, the overall and incremental benefit/cost ratios are computed, as shown in Table 5-18. Under each percentage rate, the lowest cost alternative is 1, and this is used in the initial comparison. The cost order of the remainder is 3, 2, 0, and comparisons are conducted in this order. It is noted that the benefit cost ratio method provides a set of decisions for project 3 for 5% and project 0 at 8% and 10%. These results are different from those of the annual-cost method but the same as those of the net present worth method. Furthermore, there is a clear influence on the benefit/cost ratio of the interest or discount rate.

The Rate of Return Method

The internal rate of return method is a relatively recent introduction in the field of transportation evaluation.[7] An internal rate of return is defined by the economist as the discount rate "at which the present value of both present and future benefits is just equal to the present value of both present and future costs."[8] The engineer defines rate of return somewhat differently. The engineer's definition of rate of return is as follows: "the rate of return method involves finding the interest rate at which two alternative solutions to an economy problem have equal annual costs or present worths. The first step is to find the rate-of-return on each proposed investment as compared with the solution that requires the least capital outlay, which often is the status quo. . . . Next the rate-of-return is computed on the *increase* in the investment between proposals having successively higher first costs."[9] The engineer's definition is unsatisfactory since it builds in an assumption that the lowest cost alternative is always economically feasible, and that no economic analysis of such an alternative is warranted. Such an assumption is not always valid, so the economist's definition is adopted in this example.

Table 5-18
Analysis for Benefit/Cost Ratio Method

	5%				8%				10%			
	0	1	2	3	0	1	2	3	0	1	2	3
Total Discounted Costs	57,739	48,360	51,323	48,922	44,374	36,999	39,366	37,675	37,892	31,514	33,592	32,247
Total Discounted Benefits	58,922	45,284	38,670	49,497	37,765	32,101	52,477	40,068	34,075	50,482	38,473	32,681
B/C Ratio	1.021	1.023	1.023	1.031	1.021	1.021	1.018	1.021	1.021	1.019	1.014	1.013
Inc. B/C	0/3		2/3	3/1	0/3		2/3	3/1	0/1		2/1	3/1
Ratio	0.957		0.831	1.754	1.017		0.944	1.046	1.03		0.95	0.79
Choice				√	√				√			

The method used is described in the following sentences. The rate of return of each alternative is computed and all alternatives are rejected that have a rate of return below the minimum deemed to be acceptable. For all those alternatives with acceptable rates of return, rates of return are computed for the increase in investment of pairs of alternatives taken in order of successively higher costs. The alternative with the lowest cost and a rate of return that is at least as high as the minimum is chosen.

The rate of return can be calculated in two different ways. The first way is known as the "Equivalent Annual Benefit and Cost Procedure" and is, mathematically, the solution for r in equation (5.34).

$$(crf_{r,n_F})(CFC_{y,0}) + CFO_{y,\bar{n}} + (crf_{r,n_V})(CVC_{y,0}) + CVO_{y\bar{n}} + CUT_{y,\bar{n}}$$
$$= BUN_{y,\bar{n}} + BUM_{y,\bar{n}} + BOM_{y,\bar{n}} \qquad (5.34)$$

The second method is the "Discounted Benefits and Cost Procedure." This is the solution for r in the equation (5.35).

$$\sum_{t=0}^{n}(pwf_{r,t})(CFC_{y,t} + CFO_{y,t} + CVC_{y,t} + CVO_{y,t} + CUT_{y,t})$$
$$= \sum_{t=0}^{n}(pwf_{r,t})(BUN_{y,t} + BUM_{y,t} + BOM_{y,t}) \qquad (5.35)$$

Both methods are correct, but the second is computationally simpler and is common practice among economists. For these reasons, this method is adopted for the example solution.

The solution process for the rate of return method is tedious and involves an iterative procedure. The method basically involves the selection of a supposed rate of return and a calculation of the discounted project costs and discounted projects benefits. If the two are equal, then the chosen discount rate is the rate of return. If not, then a new estimate has to be made, and the calculations repeated. This is repeated further until the rate of return is determined. This determines the rate of return for each project. Subsequently, the same process has to be adopted for the incremental costs and benefits of successively higher cost alternatives. As before, this procedure is examined for the example used in the previous sections of this chapter.

The results of the procedure are shown in Table 5-19. The rates of return of the four projects are 105%, 24.5%, 17.2%, and 13.3% respectively. The incremental rates of return are 8.3% between projects 3 and 1, 9.3% between 3 and 2, and 7.2% between 3 and 0. Hence, at 5% the decision is in favor of project 3, and at 8% and 10% it is in favor of project 0.

For a similar analysis, it can be noted that, since in this example net present worth is always positive, the rates of return for each project are acceptable for any minimum rate of return $\leq 10\%$. In this case, the calculation of overall rates of return for the projects could have been dispensed

Table 5-19
Results of Rate of Return Method

Project	5%	8%	10%
1	yes	yes	yes
2	yes	yes	no
3	no	no	no
0	no	yes	no
Decision	3	0	0

with since all are acceptable against the discount rates previously used. In the previous analyses, the lowest cost alternative is project 1. The next lowest is project 3, then project 2, and finally project 0. Clearly, the full set of computations are tedious without a preprogrammed computer, so it is worthwhile to consider whether there is an alternative to carrying out these calculations of rate of return.

Since rate of return implies a balancing of costs and benefits, it is clear that if, at some percentage interest, the benefits exceed the costs, then the rate of return is higher than that percentage interest. This follows because all benefits are discounted, while only part of the costs are discounted. In order to reduce the benefits, a higher discount rate would be chosen and this would decrease benefits more rapidly than costs. Similarly, it is clear that if costs exceed benefits at some given discount rate, then that discount rate is higher than the rate of return. Hence, in the same way that net present worth could be used to indicate an acceptable rate of return for any single project, it can also be seen that if the net present worth *increases* from one project to another, then it follows that the incremental rate of return is higher than the discount rate in question. To determine the results of the rate of return method, Table 5-17 needs to be examined for the results of the net present worth method. Comparing projects to the next lowest acceptable cost alternative, starting with the lowest cost, the results are given in Table 5-19. In this table, "yes" indicates a rate of return that is higher than the interest rate at the top of the column of the table. The decision is in favor of alternative 3 at 5% and of alternative 0 at 8% and 10%, as determined from the full calculations, but without the necessity for them.

Summary and Critique

First, the results of the various techniques may be summarized for the three interest rates selected for study. This summary is shown in Table 5-

Table 5-20
Summary of Results

Method	5%	8%	10%
Annual Costs	1	1	1
Net Present Worth	3	0	0
Benefit cost Ratio	3	0	0
Rate of Return	3	0	0

20. It is clear from the analysis that annual costs will give different results from any of the other three methods, in terms of both the best alternative and a ranking of alternatives that are less than best. The other three methods have, in this instance, agreed on best alternatives. It is also evident that the first three techniques are very sensitive to the chosen discount rate, while rate of return is very sensitive to the discount rate determined as being the acceptable minimum. The rate of return method, however, produces *information* for the decision maker that does not vary with discount rate, while the other three methods clearly give information based on an assumed discount rate.

Finally, in terms of general criticism, the four techniques must all be faulted on the grounds that they can only be used to assess projects in terms of monetary costs and benefits and those additional costs and benefits that are readily reducible to monetary terms. Thus, the decisions generated *directly* by these techniques cannot take into account the comparative amounts of irreducible costs and benefits. Instead, it is left to the decision maker to add weighted considerations of such costs and benefits to the economic information yielded by these analysis techniques. The problems that arise from this are manifold. In particular, however, there is the problem that certain nonmonetary costs and benefits are implicitly included in the analysis with implied weights. The decision maker may not be aware of the inclusion of these items and, even if he is, may find it very difficult to relate these implied weights to his subjective judgment of the alternatives. It is also clear that, because subjective weightings must be used in the decision process, there is necessarily a lack of consistency in the alternatives adopted.

Each of the four methods can also be considered separately. However, the earlier comments on the annual-cost method suggested that this method has little practical value as an evaluation technique, and so it may be concluded that the annual-cost method should be rejected as an alternative technique. Hence, detailed comparative criticisms of the techniques will be confined to the remaining three techniques.

The Benefit/Cost Ratio

Of the three techniques considered, the benefit/cost ratio method is probably the least desirable method for several reasons. First, the method is largely confined to application in highway engineering and water resources. It is likely, therefore, that the technique will not be well understood by the decision or policy makers.

Second, the use of a benefit/cost ratio is ambiguous and of problematical relative significance. It is somewhat arbitrary to reject any project with B/C ratio less than unity. Also, what is the significance of the difference between two alternatives with B/C ratios of 1.05 and 1.10? In the example already used the B/C ratios differed by not more than 0.01 between projects. It is not easy to grasp what these differences imply in terms of the relative worthwhileness of two projects.

Third, there is some arbitrariness in the treatment of certain elements of costs and benefits to be included in the computations of a benefit/cost ratio. For instance, the earlier example treated cost savings as negative costs. They could also be treated as positive benefits. If moved from the denominator to the numerator, such cost items will radically change the benefit/cost ratio computed without changing the decision set. There is no clear rule as to which is the correct way of handling such items.

On the basis of these objections, it appears to be better to reject the benefit/cost ratio method, unless remaining techniques have more serious problems attached.

Rate of Return Method

The internal rate of return method has some clear advantages over benefit/cost ratios, but also has certain problematical disadvantages. In terms of its advantages, the rate of return method is much more widely understood in business circles, and is therefore likely to be of more ready use to the decision maker than the B/C ratio. Second, it is clear that the rate of return method is not sensitive to some internally determined market discount rate. For this reason, and because of the lack of an arbitrary standard (such as a B/C ratio of 1.0), the results presented to the decision maker from use of the rate of return method are not affected by any arbitrary internal decisions, which may be unknown to the decision maker.

These advantages notwithstanding, the rate of return method has a number of problems associated with it. First, in the solution for the rate of return, situations can arise in which there is no unique solution for the rate of return. In situations where costs and benefits do not produce steadily decreasing net present values, at least two rates of return may satisfy the mathematical equation that expresses the solution method. Hence, the rate of return method can produce ambiguous results.

Second, the rate of return method is computationally tedious and inefficient. It requires a lengthy trial-and-error solution procedure. Third, serious problems arise when the alternatives considered have different service lives or terminal dates. In order to handle these problems, it is necessary that all alternatives are considered for the same analysis time period, and reinvestment of the earnings generated in the analysis period must be correctly accounted for. Problems concerning reinvestment are dealt with in *Traffic Systems Analysis* by Wohl and Martin. In summary, the problems concern the fact that reinvestment is handled implicitly in the rate of return method unless explicit attempts are made to adopt a specific policy. The handling of reinvestment is likely to play a significant role in the determination of the rate of return, and the implied assumption in many cases is invalid. This implied assumption is that "the reinvestment rate of all earnings or funds freed prior to the terminal date of the longer-lived project will be higher than the cost of capital."[10]

In general, it would appear that the rate of return method has some definite advantages over the benefit/cost ratio method, but at the same time has several problems associated with it.

Net Present Worth Method

It is readily apparent that the net present worth method and the rate of return method have some considerable similarities. In general, if all the alternatives have the same service life, the two methods will yield identical results. The net present worth method has the advantage of yielding a readily understandable result, although of a little less familiarity than the rate of return result.

The net present worth method yields unambiguous answers, and these answers are readily understandable as comparative measures. Computationally, it is much simpler than either benefit cost or rate of return, and in fact both of these latter methods require the same computations initially as those forming the total computations for the net present worth method. This method, however, does not present problems with reinvestment, and a different assumption from that of the rate of return method is implied in this method. Again, these problems are detailed in *Traffic Systems Analysis* and will not be dealt with here.

In general, it may be concluded that the best of the four techniques examined is the net present worth method. It is the method least liable to ambiguities. It produces information that can be readily understood by the decision or policy maker and is least likely to cause serious problems arising from implied assumptions. Also, the method is computationally the simplest.

6

The Identification, Measurement, and Interpretation of Impact

Introduction

The issue of identification and measurement of impacts due to changes in the transportation system is the central issue of concern when transportation-system evaluation is the topic. Because, after all, what else is it that constitutes transportation-system evaluation, but the consideration of impacts for various transportation-system alternatives on users and non-users of the respective alternatives?

In the age of increased consciousness of the state and development of the environment, the identification, measurement, and interpretation of impacts has become more and more significant in transportation planning. Previous chapters have discussed underlying economic and conceptual principles and guidelines for evaluation. This chapter develops a framework for identifying, measuring, and analyzing impacts related to changes in transportation facilities and operations.

If transportation is considered as a system, impact can be defined as the array of interactions between this system and all other systems. Thus, there is a human system, an urban system, a rural system, a natural environmental system, etc., and there are interactions between the transportation system and all of the other systems. The study of impacts is, therefore, the study of these interactions.

Until rather recently, work on transportation impacts has concentrated on highway transportation. A number of reasons can be put forth to explain this fact. First, the consciousness that there are interactions between transportation and the rest of the environment has been relatively recent. Second, major transportation-system improvements have concentrated largely on the highway mode. Third, environmental legislation requiring detailed impact statements for any federally funded or subsidized transportation project is of very recent vintage.

Given the fact that by far the largest part of transportation construction in the past has been highway-oriented, it is logical that the discussion of impacts presented in this chapter concentrates on highway-related transportation systems. This is simply a reflection of the fact that most research has been performed in this area and, consequently, that these impacts have been subjected to more intensive study. It is clear that the approach to impact identification and measurement is transferable to other types of transportation-system changes.

User and Nonuser

Traditionally, highway planning has been concerned primarily to evaluate impacts, or consequences, affecting users of the facility. The extension of considerations to nonusers is a very recent development. Assuming that the dichotomy of users and nonusers is a valid one, it becomes necessary to define each of the two categories. This immediately leads to several problems of definition.

The first question which arises is that of identifying the user. Traditional highway planning has largely defined the user as being the person who will actually travel on the proposed facility. This is sufficient if the aim is to evaluate the consequences only in the framework of a specific plan. Dichotomy of users and nonusers, however, presumably serves the function of establishing a framework for identifying consequences. It should, therefore, be meaningful in terms of identifying a dichotomy of types of consequences. In the following hypothetical situation, though, this dichotomy is not readily visible. The assumed problem is to evaluate the effects of the construction of a freeway between points A and B. It is assumed that two arterial highways run parallel to this freeway within a corridor of 2-3 miles width, and that some 6 or 7 arterials running perpendicular to this freeway are connected to it via complete interchanges.

Under these circumstances, it may reasonably be expected that travel on the parallel arterials decreases, while travel on the crossing arterials increases. Travelers on all of the arterials and the new freeway will, therefore, experience changes in overall travel times, speeds, and congestion. Traditionally, though, users are defined as those individuals or groups using the planned facility.

By similar reasoning, the nonusers are those not using the planned transportation facilities. For nonusers, consequences or impacts will be the entire spectrum of consequences on nontransportation aspects of the environment, as well as concomitant transportation consequences. Clearly, this dichotomy is not one that applies in absolute terms to any single individual. A large population close to a transportation facility will be both users and nonusers under this definition. This does not invalidate the basic definition, which does produce a clear framework within which to examine impacts.

User Impacts

In general, user impacts are those impacts or consequences of a plan that result in changes in travel times, speeds, congestion, and accident rates. As was discussed earlier, studies of highway benefits generally have been concerned with travel times and accidents. User costs, therefore, are defined as running costs of the vehicle plus travel time plus accident likelihood times the cost of an accident, plus terminal costs.

Studies of vehicle operating costs are carried out from time to time, and are usually based on a number of elements of costs. These include vehicle depreciation on a per-mile basis; maintenance costs similarly prorated, together with periodic replacement costs such as batteries, tires, etc; and gasoline and oil costs per mile. Travel time is computed on the basis of average speed and converted to a cost using a value of travel time, as indicated in chapter 4.

Finally, estimates are made of the likely reduction in accidents per vehicle-mile, resulting from the proposed improvement. Various studies have been carried out to place a cost on accidents, particularly those leading to the loss of human life.

The techniques used to calculate the value of a human life follow a variety of approaches.[1] A commonly used method is that of computing this value by means of net discounted earned income. The advocates of this approach generally concur that the market wage rate is to be used as the measure of value of output. They further agree that "unearned incomes do not measure the value of output of those who receive them."[2]

Other techniques proposed for relating the economic costs of fatal accidents to the value of work output by those involved use gross discounted wages, net discounted average output, or gross discounted average output. The different methods can result in significantly different values of life. This variation in results can obviously affect the justification for or against the construction or improvement of a transportation facility, dependent on the anticipated number of lives saved and the method of computation used.

Aside from the validity of the computational structure, there remains the morally questionable position of placing a monetary value on a human life. Since accident prevention has to be a very significant consideration in evaluating alternative transportation proposals, the analyst has no choice but to sidestep the philosophical issue and concentrate on the meaningful computation of savings related to reduced numbers of accidents.

Thus, as was already observed, user costs are evaluated entirely from impacts that can be given a monetary equivalent. Specifically, they are impacts that can be identified as a result of the change of travel conditions due to the proposed change in the facility. In general, these impacts are evaluated only for the users of the facility that is the subject of the plans. Reductions or increases in traffic on nearby facilities are not usually included, nor is the elimination or reduction of accidents on nearby facilities calculated. For a full spectrum of consequences, it is clear that these impacts should be evaluated.

Nonuser Impacts

On the basis of the previously proposed dichotomy, the nonuser impacts are those that affect people and the environment, but do not present direct consequences to people using the facility. These are the economic, social, and environmental impacts on the people, land uses, and environment adjacent to a transportation facility. Primarily, transportation facilities are provided to improve or create accessibility for people to some set of desired attractions and for goods to some set of markets or manufacturing industries. In the past, this was the only aspect of transportation-facility provision considered in the planning process. However, it has long been recognized that subsidiary effects are caused, and that the creation or improvement of accessibility results in an increase in trip making that is rarely envisioned at the planning stage.[3]

The final aim of studies on these impacts is to be able to reach the point where the full spectrum of consequences of a specific plan for the provision of a transportation facility can be predicted. Currently, this capability does not exist. As a consequence, the discussions in this chapter are directed towards the identification of impacts and the discussion of the methods, tools, and techniques that might profitably be brought to bear to permit the evaluation and prediction of impacts.

It is quite common that a rather narrow view of transportation facility impacts is taken due to the typically localized nature of the size of the facility and of the area of concern. It is appropriate, therefore, to step back for a moment and look at the broader range and more profound impacts that transportation-system changes have had on the development patterns of cities in general.

Most of the major cities in North America, and more particularly in Europe, show a growth pattern derived largely from transportation.[4] Before the days of mechanized travel, most of the cities were comparatively small and very densely developed. The distance from residential to business areas would be little more than five miles or so—about thirty minutes to one hour's horse or horse-and-carriage ride. The advent of the steam locomotive had a radical effect on these cities. Railroads were built to connect city center to city center. As a consequence, a radial pattern of railroads emerged, converging on the central city. This rapidly gave rise to the development of suburbs along the railroads, and the provision of intermediate stations to serve these suburbs. As time went by, these pockets of development gradually were linked along the railroads, forming a radial pattern of suburbs emanating from each city.

With the advent of the internal-combustion engine, it was no longer so important to be in proximity to the railroad stations. Highways were built, originally to connect urban areas, and also later to connect suburbs peripherally. Wherever these highways were built, and where distances from an existing commercial center allowed a reasonable travel time, development also spread outward from the radial rail routes to fill in the intervening spaces. As a result, the city changed from a dense core with radiating corridors of development to a continuously developed area with a roughly circular plan, modified by topography, city age, extent of planning controls, and local aberrations.

The subsequent development of arterials and expressways brought about further extended corridors of development, markedly wider than the corridors that developed along the railroad routes. Now, continued addition to and improvement of both highway and railroad facilities bring further extensions to the urban area of most of the major cities. In certain cities, the development of the urban area and the transportation system have not necessarily occurred in the order just indicated. Residential development sometimes occurs first and brings with it a demand for extended transportation systems. Most often, however, they occur in the reverse sequence, and the development patterns can be interpreted as an impact of the transportation systems. For instance, in London, one of the subway lines was extended into open country and farmland. Within less than five years, the area was a thriving suburban center.[5]

Thus, it is clear that there has been a considerable link between transportation-development patterns and urban development. This is obviously one impact of transportation that is not a user impact.

The Legal Background

Starting in 1968 a number of significant pieces of federal legislation have been passed which establish directives for the consideration and evaluation of impacts related to any federally-funded project. The National Environmental Policy Act (NEPA) of 1969 constitutes the basic legislation affecting all federal agencies involved in the sponsorship of construction or operations that might have impacts on the environment.

Section 102(2)(C) of the NEPA of 1969 calls for the preparation of an environmental impact statement, mandating that, before any federal action is taken, a statement be prepared which will describe in detail:

  (i) the environmental impact of the proposed action,
 (ii) any adverse environmental effects that cannot be avoided should the proposal be implemented,
(iii) alternatives to the proposed action,
 (iv) the relationship between local short-term uses of man's environment and the maintenance and enhancement of long-term productivity,
  (v) any irreversible and irretrievable commitments of resources which would be involved in the proposed action should it be implemented.

Section 102(2)(B) of the NEPA of 1969 makes it the responsibility of all agencies of the U.S. federal government to:

(B) identify and develop methods and procedures, in consultation with the Council on Environmental Quality, which will insure that presently unquantified environmental amenities and values may be given appropriate consideration in decision making along with economic and technical considerations.

In the transportation sector, major national concern with the consequences of transportation-system changes was first reflected in the Federal-Aid Highway Act of 1968 (23 U.S.C. 128). Under the joint authority of this Act and the Department of Transportation Act of 1966 (49 U.S.C.), the U.S. Department of Transportation, through the Federal Highway Administration, issued a Policy and Procedure Memorandum (PPM) 20-8, whose two purposes were:

a. . . . to ensure, to the maximum extent practicable, that highway locations and designs reflect and are consistent with Federal, State, and local goals and objectives. The rules, policies and procedures established by this PPM are intended to afford full opportunity for effective public participation in the consideration of highway location and design proposals . . .

b. The PPM requires State Highway Departments to consider fully a wide range of factors in determining highway locations and highway designs . . . it provides for a two-hearing procedure . . . to give all interested persons an opportunity . . . to express their views . . . when the flexibility to respond to these views still exists.[6]

It is indicated that federal aid will not be forthcoming, nor federal approval given, to projects that fail to observe the PPM. Later in the document, some of the factors to be considered in the location process are listed:

'Social, economic, and environmental effects' means the direct and indirect benefits or losses to the community and to highway users. It includes all such effects that are relevant and applicable to the particular location or design . . . such as:

1. Fast, safe and efficient transportation
2. National defense
3. Economic activity
4. Employment
5. Recreation and parks
6. Fire protection
7. Aesthetics
8. Public utilities
9. Public health and safety
10. Residential and neighborhood character and location
11. Religious institutions and practices
12. Conduct and financing of government (including effect on local tax base and social service costs)
13. Conservation (including erosion, sedimentation, wildlife and general ecology of the area)

14. Natural and historic landmarks
15. Noise, and air and water pollution
16. Property values
17. Multiple use of space
18. Replacement housing
19. Education (including disruption of school district operations)
20. Displacement of families and businesses.

Naturally, a number of additional legal directives and acts have followed since 1968, identifying a wider range of concerns and adding greater specificity to earlier legislative requirements with respect to environmental impacts of transportation projects. Most notable among this legislation is the Federal-Aid Highway Act of 1970, as implemented by FHWA Policy and Procedure Memorandum 90-4. Section 9 requires the development of so-called "Action Plans." These Action Plans are designed to detail responsibilities and procedures with respect to the identification of social, economic, and environmental consequences of transportation plans. The Action Plans are to ensure high technical quality of impact statements. Further, they are designed to make certain that all information related to the impacts of transportation projects:

(a) is developed in parallel with alternatives and related engineering data, so that the development and selection of alternatives and other elements of technical studies can be influenced appropriately;
(b) indicates the manner and extent to which specific groups and interests are beneficially and/or adversely affected by alternative proposed highway improvement;
(c) is made available to other agencies and to the public early in studies;
(d) is developed with participation of staffs of local agencies and interested citizens;
(e) is developed sufficiently to allow for the estimation of costs, financial or otherwise, of eliminating or minimizing identified adverse effects.

The above samples of general and transportation-specific Federal legislation should be sufficient to indicate the legal requirements concerning the study of transportation-system impacts. The legally-inclined reader is referred to the following legislation for further study of impact-related legal requirements:

1. The Federal Aid Highway Acts of 1962 and 1973
2. The Department of Transportation Act of 1966, Section 4(f)
3. The Civil Rights Acts of 1964 and 1968
4. The Clean Air Act of 1970
5. The National Historic Preservation Act of 1966
6. The Uniform Relocation Assistance and Real Property Acquisition Policies Act of 1970

Impact Taxonomy

As was discussed earlier in this chapter, the basic categorization of impacts relates to user and nonuser impacts. A substantial level of disaggregation can be applied in order to subdivide these impacts into a great number of more specific subimpacts. Table 6-1 shows an example of very fine subdivisions related to transportation impact (Manheim, et al., 1975).[7] Manheim, et al., identified the following main impact types:

1. Operational impacts
2. Activity-distribution impacts
3. Monetary impacts
4. Social impacts
5. Environmental impacts
6. Aesthetic impacts
7. Institutional impacts

It is evident from an inspection of Table 6-1 that the user impacts discussed earlier in this chapter are all subsumed under the heading "operational impacts," while the nonuser impacts fall under the remaining six major categories. Clearly, there are a number of possible ways to subdivide user and nonuser impacts, dependent on the analyst's disciplinary background and outlook, or the purpose of the specific classification scheme.

For purposes of discussion, the remainder of this chapter concentrates on nonuser impacts and subsumes all such impacts under the categories of economic, social, and environmental impacts. Briefly, these are defined in the following ways: economic impacts are those consequences that result in a change in the economic status of people and businesses. They are largely consequences that should be measurable in monetary terms. Social impacts are those consequences that result in changes in habits and lifestyles of people and communities and also those that affect the organization of various public institutions, such as schools, government, etc. Environmental impacts are those that affect other systems or are indirect effects on the human system. They include effects on the general ecology, air pollution, water pollution, noise, etc.

The boundaries between the impact categories occasionally become indistinct or ambiguous because of the overlapping nature of some impacts. Under those circumstances, the discussion of impacts proceeds within whichever category appears to be most suitable.

The method of addressing impacts in each of the three categories of impacts is as follows: to identify and define the specific types of impact; to describe the forms they will take; and to discuss the methods by which

Table 6-1
Impact Types

	Operational Impacts				
				Service by Mode	
Network	Facility	Accessibility		User	Goods
Network Integration	Short Run Operating Conditions	Public Services		Total Trip Speed	Goods Distribution
System Operation	Long Run Operating Conditions	Jobs		Travel Time	Freight Costs
Effect on Arterial and Local Street Systems	Relation to Future Technology Plans and Development	Recreation		Trip Length	Delivery Services
Safety	Safety	Commercial Industry		Accident Record	Terminal Location and Operation
	Modal Coordination	Churches		Operating Cost	
		Medical		Trip Reliability	
		Shopping		Comfort, Convenience & Other Qualitative Factors	
		Cultural		Level of Service	
		Friends		Usage	
		Relatives		Parking	
		Social Services			

Activity Distribution Impacts		
Land Use	Development Type	Development Opportunities
Parkland	Population	Joint Development
Open Space	Employment	Short Term
Residential	Industry	Long Term
Commercial	Production	Rezoning
Industrial	Markets	Capital Program
Institutional		

Table 6-1 (cont.)

Monetary Impacts

Agency Costs	User Costs	Neighborhood Costs	Community Costs	Displacee Costs
Right-of-Way	Operating	Property Values	Income	Replacement Costs
Construction	Maintenance	Rents	Production Value	Mortgages and
Auxiliary Facilities	Parking	Assessments	Jobs	Investments
Replacement Housing	Insurance	Taxes	Taxes Assessment	Rents
Replacement of	Accident	Pollution	Provision of	Title Fees
Facilities	Time	Blight	Services	Moving Expenses
Maintenance	Fares	Accessibility	Regional Economy	Clientele Loss or
Revenue Sources				Gain
Relocation Services				
Cost of Capital				

Social Impacts

Community Boundaries	Community Character	Community Function	Community Economy	Community Accessibility
Religious	Cohesion & Stability	Safety	Housing Supply	Church
School	Structure	Housing Quality	Employment	School
Political Ward	Identity	Public Services	Land Values	Entertainment
Ethnic District	Goals	Employment Levels	Zoning	Friends
Neighborhood	Attitudes	Industrial and		Relatives
	Population	Farming Processes		Shopping
	Composition	Pedestrian Circu-		Recreation
		lation		Parks
				Jobs
				Community Services

Environmental Impacts

Effects of Traffic		Effects of Roadway Structure	
Air Pollution	Noise	Water	Natural Resources
Real Estate Values	Psychological Effects	Drainage	Natural Resources
Material Deterioration	Ability to Concentrate	Diversion	Animal Life
Power Demands	Sleep	Erosion	Animal Migratory Paths
Mental Depression	Nuisance	Access to Light	Plant Life
Balance of Nature			Cultivated Areas
Dust			Uncultivated Areas
			Access to Light
			Glare
			Soils
			Energy Consumption

Aesthetic Impacts

View of the Facility	View From the Facility	Natural Beauty
Lighting	Location	Open Spaces
Dark Areas	Perception Sequence	Greenery
Cold Light	Design	Park System
Monotony	Rhythm	Boulevards or Gardens
Location	Signing	Lakes
Obstruction of Sunlight		Wildlife Habitats
Change of Air Currents		
Visual Barrier		
Architectural Quality		
Image—Ability		
Dimensional Balance		
Beauty		
Orientation		
Psychological Barrier		

Table 6-1 (cont.)

	Institutional Impacts		
Administrative		Community	
Governmental	Private	Historical Sites	Cultural Sites
Budgets	Educational		
Revenues	Religious		
Commitments	Military		
Priorities	Corporate		
Laws	Industrial		
Ordinances			
By Laws			
Goals and Programs			
(National Defense,			
Conservation,			
Recreation, etc.)			
Regional Access			

Source: Manheim, M.L., et al., NCHRP Report 156 (1975).

these impacts may be assessed in the framework of an attempt to predict them and to enumerate their consequences on a community.

One of the major reasons for attempting to assess these consequences is to be able to use this information as an aid to determining the optimal location and operation of a proposed transportation facility. A second objective could be to determine whether such a facility should be provided at all. It is, therefore, necessary to attempt to identify a relevant societal-value system that can be applied to these consequences.

Economic Impacts

Description of Economic Impacts

Of the three basic nonuser impact categories, economic impacts are the most clearly definable. Three major aspects of economic impact can be identified: change in accessibility of land or development, and hence a change of value; change in the type of land use; and relocation of existing land uses. None of these three basic impacts can be classified as necessarily "all good" or "all bad."

Three major aspects of economic impact have already been identified. The first of these aspects concerns the effects on property and land values of changes in accessibility. The provision of a freeway or a transit line will have two distinct impacts in terms of accessibility. Property near intersections or stations will usually benefit from increased accessibility. At locations between intersections or stations, accessibility will sometimes remain unchanged, although, depending upon provisions of cross-access, it is a frequent occurrence that property in these latter locations suffers a reduction of accessibility.

Understandably, a value system currently exists in our society that places a premium on property that has a high accessibility. In the case of residential property, high access means ease of travel to work, shopping, recreation, school, social, and other activity centers. For commercial and industrial land uses, accessibility means ease of access for employees and supplies. In the case of commercial development, it also means ease of access for the market (i.e., individual purchasers of items, representatives of firms, etc.), while for industrial development, it means ease of egress for distribution to market outlets. For these various reasons, such land uses obtain economic benefits from increased accessibility. In the case of commercial and industrial development, these benefits may result in improved turnover and hence bigger profits. In all cases, they will probably be seen as increases in the market value of the property.

In the case of farmland, social, recreational, and religious activity centers, the results of higher accessibility will often be higher utilization of the land and also possibly a reduction in maintenance overheads due to a general improvement of access to services and labor for upkeep of the activity center.

Similarly, for all these existing land uses, decreases in accessibility have the potential to be economically damaging. Property values may be lowered, existing markets either diverted elsewhere or maintained only at increased expense, and so forth. These can be identified as the principal economic impacts on existing land uses of the provision of a new transportation facility. As a subset of this, a principal economic link between accessibility and individuals can also be identified.

By far the greatest proportion of employed people perceive a physical limitation on their job opportunities in terms of accessibility between their current residential area and prospective employment locations. These limitations also exist in terms of the communication media through which vacancies or employment opportunities are advertised. The professional and managerial classes, for whom potential job locations are probably advertised at least nationally, if not internationally, are only a relatively small minority of the total labor force. Thus, a change in accessibility can also result in a change in potential job opportunities for an individual, and consequently a change in rate of advancement. This illustrates an economic impact on individuals as a result of a transportation facility.

The second area of economic impacts concerns a change of land use as a result of changed accessibility. This can occur in a number of ways. For example, a new facility might isolate a small tract of farmland or vacant land between itself and a developed area. As a consequence both of the separations of such an area and the proximity of a transportation facility, this land may be developed for commercial, industrial, or residential uses. A further effect of this situation is a considerable rise in the value of the land. This rise in value is considerably greater for unimproved lots than for existing property developments. Another way in which a change in land use may occur is in the case of land already developed that exists in specified locations with respect to the new facility. Decreases in the accessibility and relative isolation of existing development may result in a gradual deterioration of the property and eventual abandonment. This is effectively a change in land use and will also result in a drop in value of the property and land.

On the other hand, property near interchanges or stations is likely to become commercially attractive. If commercial use is not currently a major land use, pressures will arise for acquisition of existing properties and conversion to commercial uses, or even a total rebuilding of the area.

These changes will also be likely to result in rising values for the property concerned. Similarly, various other existing developments may be acquired to allow expansion or location of land uses such as industrial development. For instance, an existing small industrial area may receive a considerable impetus for expansion as a result of the construction of a new transportation facility. This impetus may result in the purchasing and redevelopment of adjacent land uses for the expansion, and may again result in increased values for the property concerned. It should also be noted, however, that the changes in land use described will have further impacts themselves on adjacent property. It should also be clear that these changes can be seen either as beneficial or detrimental, depending upon viewpoint.

The final major area of economic impact is that of relocation. At this point, only the economics of relocation are considered and some of the other aspects are left to later sections of this chapter. Relocation will normally result from the alignment of the right-of-way where the purchase and demolition of all property within that right-of-way is required. Because of this, two economic impacts are generated: the cost to the developer of acquiring properties, and the cost to the resident or user in relocating and adapting to a new environment. It needs to be stated at this point that such relocation is not always necessarily an economic loss to the individual. Forced relocation of residences has frequently been shown to result in a raising of the living standard of those affected and the purchase of a higher quality house. Similarly, the effects on nonresidential uses can often be stimulating, resulting from the opening up of new markets, the precipitation of needed modernization of equipment and reorganization, etc. In terms of residential areas, it can also be a means of aiding slum clearance and rehousing; while with other developments it can also lead to the replacement of outmoded, unsafe, or otherwise substandard property by new and improved buildings.

On the other hand, this relocation can bring economic hardship, as well as other undesirable consequences. Rehousing may force people to rent or buy property that is more expensive because there is no other property available. Similarly, some rehousing schemes, particularly those related to slum clearance, often do no more than create new slums—usually vertical ones instead of horizontal.[8] Small firms—commercial and industrial—are particularly susceptible to relocation. It may often result in the reduction of markets, and require investment in overly expensive property. These effects will often result in the firms going out of business.

Several major economic impacts have been identified. The next task is to consider how this identification can be used as a basis for evaluating the benefits and disbenefits of the facility.

Evaluation of Economic Impacts

In terms of changed values of property, there appear to be two basic requirements for analysis and evaluation. The first is to determine the
changes in accessibility that will occur; and the second is to determine the
economic value of such changes. This sounds relatively simple. However,
the definition of accessibility is not clear, and its evaluation is even more
complex. First, the evaluation of economic impacts requires an analysis
of the trip patterns centered on the property concerned. With this knowledge, in addition to information on route and mode choices of these trips,
some estimate may be made of the changes in accessibility and of the proportion of trips that will be affected. By studying the effects on property
values of past transportation improvements, it should then be possible to
evaluate the actual economic benefits or detriments of the facility to each
property. Many studies have attempted to aggregate properties and determine average changes in values without recourse to a study of changes in
accessibility. The results have invariably been difficult to assess. In addition, of course, the changes in property values are likely, particularly in
the case of residential property, to be due to many more factors than just a
change in accessibility. The aesthetics and environmental impacts of the
facility are also typically reflected in value changes. Another difficulty
likely to be encountered in this type of analysis concerns the problems of
obtaining information on "before" and "after" values and relating these
changes to a "norm." It is likely that a study of such changes would have
to be conducted almost entirely for major facilities, where the potential
impacts should affect a large number of properties, and with the use of a
control area to determine the natural price trends. These are just a few
ideas of the approach and methodology that appears to be indicated for
this evaluation.

The evaluation of changes in land uses is likely to be even more complex. Given that the location of probable changes can be determined, the
economic effects will not present much difficulty for evaluation. The identification of such locations is much more problematical. One approach
that can be taken is to study past installation of new facilities and identify
the locations where changes in land use have occurred. Such studies have
already suggested that the areas around intersections or stations are prone
to land-use changes. Thus, interchanges on a freeway generate service
stations, eating facilities, motels, and similar land uses. Transit stations
often generate parking areas and small retail establishments such as drug
stores, together with increased development intensity for residential uses
nearby. A number of studies have been concerned with attempts to predict the likely extent and economic impact of these specific developments. However, the wider land-use changes that may result from the
building of a new facility present greater difficulty for analysis and predic-

tion. It can be predicted safely that interchanges or stations will generate changes in existing land-use patterns, although their extent, value, and wider impacts are much less easily handled. Beyond that, the identification of the locations of other probable changes is a problem.

It is also worth noting that some of the changes discussed in this section can come about only through local government action. Changes in land use will largely only follow on changes in zoning and annexation of unincorporated land. Both of these are processes that occur through the political machinery of villages, towns, and cities affected by a particular facility. The major effect here is one of increasing the pressure for growth, which results in a demand for changes in zoning and in community boundaries. Thus, in this respect at least, communities have some say in determining the extent of land-use changes that will occur.

Since much of this discussion has been concerned with the negative impacts, it may also be noted that with respect to the above comments, the location of a transportation facility can have beneficial results. The following example from northern Illinois will illustrate this point. One village in this area is somewhat exceptional in that it has basically only two types of zoning—5-acre residential lots and 1-acre residential lots. It is an area in which most of the people are relatively wealthy. The village wants to retain its present zoning, but is under considerable pressure from neighboring communities who want to edge into the village and zone at 2-4 houses per acre. Based on past experience and some studies, it appears likely that a freeway located to the west and north of the village, between it and several communities of denser development who want to expand towards the village, would constitute a barrier to zoning changes. It is usually expensive to extend drainage systems, utilities, and other necessities for residential and commercial development across a freeway already constructed. In this way, the freeway can provide a barrier that the other communities will be reluctant to cross, and will, therefore, remove pressures on the village to change its zoning.

Finally, the evaluation of the economic impacts of relocation have to be considered. Before discussing these relocation impacts, it is worthwhile to look briefly at the process of land acquisition by a state or municipality. This process is based on the principle of "eminent domain." This means that a state or municipality has the right to "condemn" property and purchase it for uses that are in the public interest. The price, however, is negotiable. The state will have the property appraised and offer this value to the owner. The owner may accept or not as he wishes. If he does not accept, he has to go to court, and the court will order him to sell. He may, however, have his own appraisal made and may contend in court that the state should pay the value stated by his appraiser. The court will then instruct the state to mediate and settle on a fair price.

In 1970, the Uniform Relocation Assistance and Real Property Acquisition Policies Act was passed. This Act ensured the removal of statutory barriers to the equitable financial reimbursements of displaced households. According to this legislation, homeowners may receive up to $15,000 above "fair market value" for the purchase of comparable decent, safe, and sanitary housing. In addition to considerations of property owners, the Act makes provisions for rental supplements to people displaced from their rented accommodations.

Prior to the 1970 Act, the Federal Aid Highway Act of 1968 had made the provision that all moving expenses be paid up to $25,000, and alternative payments made to a business that cannot relocate. In addition, the Act required the assurance of an adequate program of relocation assistance and availability of relocation housing before approval is given of any highway project. The value of reimbursements requires separate state legislation. To induce the enactment of such state laws, the Highway Act provided for 100% reimbursement from federal funds of payments made before 1970. After 1970, federal participation was set to occur on a project basis.

Thus, a homeowner can receive "fair market value" for his home, and between nothing and $1,000 relocation expenses, depending upon the state he lives in, and the amount of his relocation expenses. A tenant, similarly, can receive relocation expenses only; and a business will receive " fair market value" for permanent property, together with relocation payments of anything up to $25,000, again depending on both the amount of expense caused and the state in which it is located.

The economics of relocation are not as simple as this analysis of reimbursement policy might suggest. In the first place, there are problems of homeowners who are still paying off a mortgage and who have to move into a house with a higher price than the current market value of their existing one. Among people faced with this situation, there are bound to be some whose age will result in most lending institutions refusing a new mortgage; there will be others whose financial status has changed since their original mortgage agreement was made with the same result; and similar problems will arise for divorcees and their families.

Similarly, a social stigma is often attached to receiving relocation help from the city or state. This often results in net deterioration in living standards for those who refuse available help but whose financial status seriously needs whatever assistance is available. Clearly, the attitudes of officials, whose task it is to take care of relocation assistance, are an important aspect of a relocation program.

Another important aspect of relocation concerns the time period over which relocation occurs. The relocation of all residents and businesses within the right-of-way of a new facility is not accomplished overnight. It is usually a protracted process which may last over a year. During this time, property is left vacant, landlords neglect maintenance requirements, and poor people are drawn to the area for temporary shelter. As a result of these changes, the area shows a marked deterioration and property values decline rapidly. This may have serious impact on the "fair market value" that can be obtained by any owner, and it also breeds many other economic and social problems. Small businesses in such an area are particularly prone to being hit by such deterioration.

The evaluation of the economic impacts of relocation cannot proceed simply by assessing the differences between total costs to each individual or business, based on prior values, and the amount of relocation payment that can be claimed. Instead, it becomes necessary to attempt to make estimates of the total impacts of relocation on property values, prior to assessment, on markets and supplies for businesses, on the ability of a business to relocate, and on the wider financial impacts of a move by an individual, family, or business. Among these latter impacts will be changes in property taxes, maintenance costs, heating costs; changes in trip patterns and acceptable trip destinations for various trip purposes; and changes in accessibility.

Basically, the tentative solutions that have been put forward here require a level of data collection and analysis far higher than anything that has been attempted outside academia so far. The expenses of such tasks, carried out on a sufficient scale, would also be considerable. Nonetheless, only one approach has been outlined through all this—the case study approach and subsequent inferential analysis. An alternative, and perhaps preferable, approach would be to attempt to hypothesize the way in which these impacts will occur and to set up evaluative techniques given the knowledge of the locations, extent, and type of the impacts (i.e., whether they are beneficial or detrimental).

Social Impacts

Definition and Identification

In any urban area, there is a continuing process of social change in much the same way that there is a continuing process of economic change. This discussion is concerned with changes over and above general changes, caused primarily by the location of a new transportation facility, or other transportation-system changes. Of specific concern is the identification of impacts on the social aspects of a community. It would be prudent to propose a definition of social impacts that could be used as a framework in which to identify such impacts. Such a definition has been put forward by

Thiel.[9] Social impacts are those influences that ". . . change the relationship between people and social institutions such as the family, community, government, schools, churches, etc."

Such impacts will result both from direct effects of the transportation facility on the land uses around it, and from indirect effects of such other facility impacts as relocation.

Effectively, the entire spectrum of interactions between the human and the physical subsystems is involved here. In order to define the social consequences of the transportation system, a definition put forward by Thomas and Schofer[10] can be useful. A few concepts which Thomas and Schofer use must be introduced. Interactions between humans as individuals or groups, and between humans and the physical subsystem can be termed "activities." Activities undertaken by individuals or groups can be termed their "activity set." Similarly, these activities may be connected to specific physical locations, which can be termed the "activity opportunities." The specific function of the transportation system is to link individuals to their activity opportunities, when these are spatially separated and when physical presence at the activity opportunity is necessary. Thus, a change in the transportation system can have impacts of two general types on the human subsystem:

(1) The activity set of the individual or group, given a fixed home base, may be altered. This may result because: (a) former activity sites have relatively greater or lesser accessibility than previously; (b) the physical attributes of the former site have become more or less suitable for the activity; (c) former activity sites have been consumed as a result of the modification of the transportation system.

(2) Individuals and groups may decide to relocate their "home bases," i.e., the sites or establishments which act as focal points for their behavioral patterns. An individual's residential site, the meeting place of a group, or the plant of a manufacturing concern, are examples of home bases. Such relocations result from the same three factors affecting changes in activity behavior patterns. Of course, the relocation of a base of operations can also be expected to result in changes in the behavior patterns—the activity sets—of individuals and groups.[11]

In order to illustrate what is meant here it is instructive to look at some instances. This in turn can lead on to a discussion of how specific consequences can be defined and measured. When the economic consequences of transportation-facility provision were discussed, it was useful to look at three basic occurrences brought about by the construction—changes in accessibility, changes in land uses, and demolition of existing buildings causing relocation. The same morphology of basic consequences can be used again for considering social consequences.

From the definition of social consequences given by Thomas and Schofer, it is obvious that the first case—change of accessibility—is an instance of (1b). There are two major categories of specific effects that may take place: the new facility acts either as an assistance to reach the required activity sites, or it acts as a barrier to reaching such places. In other words, the existing activity linkages are changed. In the event that no linkages are disrupted, and some are even improved, changes may still occur in the activity sets of those concerned. If total travel for the various activities is reduced, then participation in the activities may be increased or an extension of the activity set may occur. The alternative occurrence is that at least some linkages of a household are disrupted. This results in either a change in the activity set, where travel times have been increased and there is a desire to maintain some of the activities affected, or the substitution, where possible, of other activity sites or even other activities, if the disruption is such that comparative travel times are greatly increased.

Changes in the activity set, or of the locations where activities are carried out, are not necessarily detrimental changes. Sometimes, such changes may have the overall effect of improving the life style of those concerned. Nevertheless, when changes occur that disrupt existing activity linkages, and where no alternative site exists, the social consequences may become very serious. Thus a coherent community may be disrupted by a highway or transit line placed through it with little or no cross-access provided. Part of the community may find itself cut off from schools, churches, social institutions, etc. This may result in either a traumatic readjustment of the life of the community, or a rapid decay of the area as a residential location. Residential communities are not alone in being affected in this way. Churches, schools, parks and other recreational facilities, shopping centers, industrial sites, etc. may all be affected by a transportation link that is imposed between it and the community, or part of the community, that it serves. The consequences of this situation will include economic ones on the actual land uses, but principally will be social consequences to the communities concerned.

The next set of social consequences can be seen as stemming from changes in land use. Such changes may result in a change of activity sets because new opportunities for certain activities are now presented, or because old opportunities have been lost. The results will look very much like those ensuing from changes in accessibility. The loss of activity sites that were important and nonsubstitutable will have serious effects on the community. Similarly, the opening up of new opportunities would usually be a beneficial effect. This might come about by the location of a new shopping plaza near a freeway, or the opening up of park or forest land for recreational purposes. Many other instances can easily be brought to mind. Change in land use where either it was formerly, or becomes subsequently, residential is effectively part of the third set of effects that will generate consequences: the effects of relocation.

The relocation of residences will have a major effect on the activity sets of the individuals involved. Relocation that takes place because of property acquisition for the construction of a right-of-way could be termed forcible relocation. This results in a not necessarily desired disruption of existing activity sets and the rebuilding of new linkages and activity locations. This effect can be particularly serious where a part of a once-coherent community is uprooted and relocated physically away from the remainder of the community to which it belongs. Often, this occurs with piecemeal urban renewal of low-income housing. Many of the original activity linkages are destroyed because of the physical separation of the parts of the community, although these linkages may be an essential part of the social structure of the community. Such relocation is disruptive and may be expected generally to have some detrimental effects on the entire community involved.

The other relocation of residences that may occur is a voluntary one, resulting possibly from the generation of new housing developments, which in turn have evolved because of the building of a new transportation facility that has made particular locations more attractive as potential housing developments. Those families that relocate in such developments are presumably doing so voluntarily and have, therefore, made a conscious decision to change the home base of their activity sets and possibly the activity sets themselves. The changes have also presumably been undergone because a net improvement in family life style is expected to result. Such location is, therefore, largely constructive and benefits those who are affected.

Relocation of other land uses largely will have the effects of changing the activity sets of those who utilize the sites before relocation and of those who may be able to use them after relocation. Two major consequences can be identified in this case. The relocation of services, e.g., doctors, dentists, and stores, will usually generate changes in the activity linkages such that those who were originally serviced by such establishments will have to seek other establishments within an acceptable journey length. On the other hand, insofar as the establishments do relocate, others may be offered greater choice of establishments from which to obtain their required services. Concomitantly, relocation of commerce or industry will affect the work trips of those involved, making them easier (shorter) or harder (longer). It will also affect potential labor markets for the activities. These changes will again affect the activity sets of the individuals concerned. More or less time may be involved in traveling to and from work with a consequent effect on the amount of time available for travel to and from, and participation in, other activities. Similarly, competition for jobs may affect job stability and anticipation of job advancement.

Many more social consequences can be identified, and many of the references for this chapter present both general and specific instances.

Measurement and Evaluation

The task of the planner is to assess the social consequences of the provision of a particular facility. These consequences have to be assessed in the framework of the questions of whether or not to build the facility and, if to build it, where specifically to locate it, i.e., how to determine the alignment of the route. As discussed previously, one major property that simplifies the assessment of economic consequences is the fact that the units of economic consequences are known. Furthermore, those units are the same as those used to assess both the money cost of constructing the facility and many of the direct user benefits of it. This property is not applicable for the assessment of social and environmental consequences. It may be possible to devise dollar equivalences of these consequences, but such measures may not necessarily be meaningful or helpful. Hence, one of the problems implicit in this evaluation is to determine a scale or system of measurement that is meaningful for evaluation purposes and that can be utilized in an overall consideration of the transportation facility.

Due to the current lack of such techniques and evaluative measures, location and routing decisions are arrived at largely through political channels. The proposal to provide a new transportation facility within a specified corridor usually has the effect of producing reactions from existing community and municipality organizations and of supplying the impetus for the formation of other groups of affected individuals. The burden of evaluating and scaling social consequences (and also certain economic and environmental consequences) is thus placed on these groups. The planning process is then such that the relative effects of the evaluation of consequences by each group are assessed in proportion to the amount of political influence of each group. Unfortunately, community groups that have no political sway, and single individuals without strong political influence, are likely to have a concomitantly slight influence on the planning process. Hence, important consequences of the planned facility may be completely ignored, and other consequences may have a distorted effect on the planning process. Thus, it appears to be desirable to develop a method of evaluation that is "absolute and impartial" as far as possible and which is independent of the level and influence of community organization.

On the basis of the discussions of the social consequences, it appears that two basic prerequisites of an evaluative method are: to identify the activity sets of households; and to determine a basis for evaluating each activity linkage in terms of its importance in the life style of the household. Before going into this in detail, a further question needs to be posed. Many studies have revealed that the average American household is very mobile. Given this level of mobility, the question arises whether changes in activity sets and the locations of sites for activities and home and workplace are significant. It is not easy to supply a definite answer to this question. However, a number of facets of this mobility can be identified that should help to indicate the probable answer. First, it is not unusual that a facility will be located through areas, generally, of low-cost housing. Typically, the residents of such housing are low-income families with a high dependence on mass transit for mobility and a strong identification with their community. The more mobile elements of society are generally of higher income groups, who do not depend on mass transit and have considerably more tenuous ties with their immediate community.

The second aspect of this argument concerns the nature of the community. Even though households may change location at fairly frequent intervals, the communities may preserve a total identity irrespective of this individual mobility. More importantly, many community groups and organizations have a stability quite independent of the rapidity of change of individuals in the community. Thus, even though churches, schools, and clubs, for example, are highly dependent upon the communities they serve, they are not very sensitive to household mobility. Finally, it appears that the social well-being of a community is largely dependent upon an established, stable set of activities and organizations in the community.

For these reasons, it appears that social consequences probably are important irrespective of the mobility of individual households. Hence, this fact leads back to the necessity of attempting to devise means of assessing the social impacts.

It is not the intention to give a detailed exposition of the techniques that have so far been proposed, but rather to introduce them in outline form and discuss them briefly. The identification of activity sets can be undertaken on the basis of past household-interview surveys for transportation studies, or by carrying out fresh and much more highly detailed surveys of the trip-making patterns of households. This form of data will allow the identification of patterns of activity linkages from communities. This is essentially the technique suggested by Ellis.[12]

Alternatively, the problem may be considered as being one of concern about the disruptive effects of locating a transportation facility through a contiguous community, termed a neighborhood. If this is so, then the identification problem is to determine the spatial boundaries of neighborhoods.[13] The major problems encountered here are those of defining a neighborhood and devising measures that will allow it to be identified. This technique is the one outlined by Hill and Frankland,[14] who find it necessary to make a series of, as yet, untested assumptions about the nature of a neighborhood. As a partial measure of a neighborhood, Hill and Frankland proposed a mobility index, which is put forward as a device that measures both the stability of an area and the propensity of the area to be stable. McGinnis[15] proposed the use of this index and three others as a partial step towards evaluating the impact of relocation. Potentially, the index can also be used to permit mapping of neighborhoods and an attempt would then be made to route new facilities along boundaries between neighborhoods. Unfortunately, it is not clear how the use of the mobility index (MI) will actually define the boundaries of neighborhoods. It is also not clear how the delineation of neighborhoods in a community can be utilized to determine the social effects of the location of a transportation facility. A possible method might be to sum the MI scores of each residential unit that will be required along a right-of-way, and also to compute the score gradients across the right-of-way and attempt to minimize the former and maximize the latter as partial criteria of location. Earlier discussions in this chapter, however, indicated that the social consequences of facility location are not limited only to a disruption of the neighborhood, but may well be caused by comparative isolation or increased accessibility of a neighborhood resulting from the presence of the facility. This seems to lead back to a consideration of the activity linkages.

Given that the data requirements of identifying activity linkages can be met within specified operational constraints, it becomes necessary to propose a rationale for the use of this information. Simplistically, a neighborhood can be defined in terms of the density of linkages between residences and activity sites. (In this case, the definition of a neighborhood is somewhat broader than that used by Hill and Frankland.[16] Instead of defining a coherent unit of residences alone, this definition specifies a coherent unit of residences and activity sites.) On the basis of the information on activity linkages, any proposed routing of the facility can be assessed in terms of the number of linkages it will destroy and the number of new linkages it will create.

This simplistic rationale has a number of problems associated with it. It is clear that the assessment of a complete route on this basis will lead potentially to a suboptimal choice of location. It would obviously be possible that the route with the lowest number of net destroyed linkages, or highest net added linkages, could be one that cuts a large number of linkages of one community while adding linkages to all the others. Therefore, its total impact may be significantly greater than other alternatives. This would not be revealed by a simple summation process. Second, this approach lends equal weight to every linkage of a community. At least two parameters may be necessary to qualify the importance of linkages: the frequency, and the substitutability of the linkage. A third, even more problematical, parameter may be needed to indicate the importance of the existence of the linkage to the social structure of the household. A further problem associated with this approach concerns the definition of the destruction or creation of a linkage. If the construction of an at-grade free-way causes the termination of a number of cross-streets, so that linkages across the line of the freeway have to be routed by a new, usually longer, route, then at what point can the linkage be considered to be cut? Similarly, the greater accessibility to other locations offered by such a freeway may be considered to add new linkages. But, how much must the accessibility be improved to define the creation of a new link?

These are a few of the problems that need to be faced before this method can be considered as a basis of evaluation. They should, however, lead to the possible refinement and development of the concept towards an operational tool. The technique is also directed more specifically to the social consequences of the construction of the facility on residences that are physically not touched by the facility. Of equal importance is the consideration of the social and community consequences of relocation.

The consequences of relocation of a section of a community can be assessed partially by an analysis of the activity linkages of both the relocated section and the section left where it was. Other measures, however, would also appear to be necessary. These are measures that would indicate whether the relocation brought about a net gain in family life style to the relocatees, and also an assessment of the net "damage" to the part of the community left behind. Equally important in this is the necessity to define "net gain in family life style." It is of small comfort to determine that the majority of relocated families improve their life style by an increased standard of housing, etc., when this has to be done at the expense of financial and social hardships, and occurs because the alternative of retaining the same life style does not exist. A number of attempts have been made to rate the effects of relocation on various categories of people. These attempts are centered around the idea of defining the vulnerability of certain groups of families to social disruption caused by relocation. The study conducted by McGinnis,[17] uses measures of mobility, social rank, urbanism, and a measure of the vacancies existing in the neighborhood that would be unaffected by right-of-way acquisition. The major problem that is encountered here, as in other similar attempts, is that of weighting the various indices to establish a relocation impact index.

Also, the relocation of work places, schools, and other major activity sites should be considered. Very little has been done to attempt to quantify the impacts of these relocations. A number of aspects need to be evaluated. The principal impact of a relocation of employment facilities is a change in employment opportunities for a segment of the population. Subsequent impacts include changes in land-use patterns and development as a direct result of the move of an existing commercial or industrial concern, and relocation of families as a reaction to changed jobs, and consequently changed residential opportunities. Quantification of these changes is difficult, and has not been attempted in detail. Similarly, the effects of relocation of schools and other major activity sets have not been investigated. Furthermore, a rationale for such investigations has not yet been proposed.

Finally, it is necessary to consider a number of institutional domains that can be affected by the location decision. First among these is the consideration of political boundaries—townships, villages, etc. There is a large measure of identification of people with their political unit, and a facility that comes between them and, say, the offices of the village board may have a disruptive effect. The difficulties of extending utilities and services across a major transportation facility were noted earlier. This will clearly have an effect on the part of a political unit left on the ''wrong'' side of the facility.

Other institutional domains that need to be considered are hospital areas, school districts, mail routes, etc. In each case, a facility can have serious disruptive effects if it tends to split parts of the domains, and also if it causes reductions in accessibility of certain parts of the domain. For instance, a small area within a school district, isolated by a facility, with reduced accessibility, may present such a problem of access for a school bus that it becomes necessary to change the school district boundaries.

Environmental Impacts

As with each of the other categories of impact, the first necessity is to define what environmental impacts are. For purposes of this discussion, environmental impacts are defined as those aspects of the consequences of construction and operation of a transportation facility that affect the physical environment, rather than land uses and social and economic aspects of life. The four principal forms of environmental impacts are identified here as those relating to ecology, noise, air, and visual (aesthetic) pollution. As was shown in Table 6-1, other types of environmental impacts exist and can be defined. This discussion, however, will focus on these four main categories without attempting to present as detailed an analysis as would be generated by a disciplinary specialist, such as an ecologist, or an air or noise pollution expert.

Identification

With the exception of the ecological effects, the specific problem is that of evaluating three physical environmental effects in order to reach some statements of impact on life. However, although these impacts are more

.ble to physical measurement than social and economic impacts, the
.nt of their impact is not measurable on the basis of such precise, abso-
measurements. Clearly, though, physical measurements of these ef-
ts of the facility constitute at least a starting point for evaluation.

Transportation facilities and operation can affect the delicate ecological balance between man on one side, and his supporting natural systems
on the other. The social and economic impacts discussed earlier and the
impacts to be discussed later in this section are all part of human ecology.

In addition to this, there are a number of other ecological impacts on
the animal and plant ecosystems. Air pollution has impacts in terms of its
effect on both plants and animals. The location of a facility such as a freeway or a transit line may interrupt the usual migratory paths of animals,
such as deer. If their paths are not blocked by fences, then many deaths
may occur as a result of animals being hit by vehicles. Similarly, the loss
of vegetation caused by the paving of the facility may disturb the ecological balance. Changes in drainage patterns, the presence of impermeable
and impervious foundation materials beneath the transportation facility,
changes of grades of the land, etc., will also tend to generate changes in
ecology. Also, the use of salt on a highway in winter can do serious damage to plant life. Sodium and chlorine ions both tend to travel through the
soil and may also damage foliage by burning.

Of the three forms of physical impact, noise has been subjected to
more experimentation and measurement than either of the other two.
Measuring noise is complicated by the fact that noise is composed of
sound pressure, frequency, and character. For this reason, it is necessary
to use various weighted scales of measurement of sound. It is not intended to go into detailed expositions of the mechanics of measurements of
noise, or of the other impacts. Instead, some of the results of such measurements and the means of interpretation will be indicated here.

Traffic noise[18] is largely a continuous, nonimpulsive noise, and this is
best measured on an "A" weighted scale of decibels (dBA). As with all
decibel scales, an increase of 10 dBA represents an approximate doubling
of loudness. Reaction to noise, however, is subjective and also related to
the amount and extent of subjection to noise during the day and night.
Hence, the impact of a new transportation facility in terms of the noise
produced will depend to a large extent on its location and on the people
who will be affected. Noise from road vehicles is made up of a number of
separate types of noise. The most serious is engine and exhaust noise,
which can be controlled, at least partially, by engine design and efficient
mufflers. Frequently, the worst offenders in terms of adherence to legal or
suggested measures of noise reduction are diesel buses and trucks. Increases in engine and exhaust noise will result from steep gradients, sharp
curves, and intersections. Two further noise sources, of particular impor-

tance on expressways, are tire noise and aerodynamic noise. Tire noise is related both to speed and surface material of the pavement. Little is known of the relationships between different pavement surface materials, speed, and noise production. Some recent experimentation has suggested that, at freeway speeds, asphalt surfaces may produce sounds of 6-10 dBA less than concrete surfaces. Full details of the experiments have not yet been released, and these are preliminary findings.[19] Aerodynamic noise is a function of both vehicle design and speed. Again, the vehicles producing the higher levels of aerodynamic noise are likely to be trucks and buses, since aerodynamic styling of autos is a good selling line and has been incorporated to varying degrees by auto manufacturers for some time.

Finally, noise is also produced by loose components of vehicles and their loads. In particular, articulated trucks and multi-axled trucks are prone to vehicle vibration noises. These noises are in part related to vehicle design and maintenance standards, in part to load-carrying design, and in part to the pavement surface. Potholes, bad patching, or a deteriorating pavement surface will cause even the best-designed, carefully loaded vehicle to emit considerable vibration noise.

Furthermore, the noise levels produced by a facility will depend to some extent on the volume of traffic. In the case of an arterial street with a 30 mph posted limit, mean noise levels double from 60 dBA to 70 dBA as volume increases from 250 vehicles per hour to 800 vehicles per hour. However, an increase to 3,000 vehicles per hour only raises mean noise levels to about 73 dBA. In the design of expressways, it is unlikely that volume of traffic will affect mean noise levels appreciably, since volumes for such facilities are almost certainly likely to exceed 1,000 vehicles per hour for most of the day and night.

Noise from other transportation facilities has been the subject of much less research.[20] Any form of fixed-rail system will tend to give rise to a more impulsive, less continuous, noise, unless the frequency of passage of vehicles and the distance from which they are audible is such that continuous noise levels are generated. This situation is unlikely to arise except very close to a major terminal facility or on the downtown section of a facility. (At an office block in Central London, situated alongside the approach to the largest London rail terminus, where twelve lines were operated, it required a train frequency of more than one every five seconds—taking all lines together—to produce a noise characteristic with some semblance of continuity.)[21] Noise sources for such facilities will tend to vary somewhat with the motive power used. In electric-traction systems, engine noise will be a source but may be less significant than other sources. Diesel engines, and other similar motive-power units will emit significant engine and exhaust noise. Here again, design can help to make significant reductions in the noise levels. A nearby station, or the presence of speed limits, or stop signals frequently requiring a train to reduce speed or stop will increase the amount of engine noise, regardless of engine type. An exception to this would be a linear-induction motor, but such motive power is not currently in use.

Other sources of noise are steel wheel on steel rail, which will depend on wheel and track design, track alignment, and track type. Short rail lengths will produce considerable noise as against continuously-welded track. Considerable gains can be made by careful design and high quality maintenance of the permanent way. Vehicle speed will also affect the level of noise production of the wheels and track. Aerodynamic noise will also occur at speed, and good design can be utilized to reduce this.

Although noise production from highway or rail vehicles is largely a function of vehicle and right-of-way design, these design features are not the specific immediate concern of the transportation planner. The propagation of the sound generated by a facility, however, is affected very considerably by the overall design and location of the facility. This will be the context in which this topic is discussed after completing the identification of the other sources of environmental impact.

Air pollution occurs as a result of both the motive power of the vehicles and the effects of wear on all moving parts. The forms of air pollution that are most noxious stem from the exhausts of gasoline and diesel engines, and comprise unburnt hydrocarbons, carbon monoxide, and nitrogen oxides. Diesel engines, by and large, emit considerably less of all three major pollutants, although diesel engines produce very significant odor pollution.[22] This odor pollution is more easily noticed than the gaseous pollutants of gasoline engines, and therefore, tends to put diesel engines in a disadvantageous position. Significantly, the automobile contributes about 82% of the carbon monoxide pollution of the atmosphere, while diesel engines contribute a fraction of the remaining 18%.[23] At all levels of operation of vehicle engines, the diesel engine emits less than 10% as much CO as the gasoline engine.[24,25] Exhausts from gasoline and diesel engines are also capable of forming ozone in the air. Ozone is also produced by the electric arcing between pick-up and power supply for electric engines. It has been demonstrated that ozone is a principal part of the oxidant characteristics of metropolitan smogs. Hence, both electric and internal combustion engines are air pollutants. A further major pollutant from the gasoline engine is lead. For many years, lead has been an additive to gasoline as an anti-knock compound. The octane rating of gasoline is a measure of the anti-knock properties, and generally octane levels above about 94 can be achieved cheaply only by the addition of lead. The lead does not undergo any chemical change in the engine and is emitted in particulate form from the exhaust. Thus, it is largely an air pollutant and settles out of the air only very gradually. So far as is known, it does not appear to form a significant hazard as a water or food pollutant.

The last few years have seen the introduction of lead-free gasolines of a substantially lower octane rating than the standard and premium grades common throughout the United States. Initially, lead-free gasoline was introduced as an attempt to reduce a recognized pollutant (lead particulates). At the time, there was little documentary evidence that the lead particulates caused physiological damage to man, or to animal or plant life. Rather, it was recognized as an obvious pollutant with clear potential danger. The introduction of lead-free gasoline required the development of a new line of automotive engines, using lower compression ratios and having concomitantly poorer power and acceleration characteristics. Subsequently, the catalytic converter was introduced for the removal of carbon monoxide. This converter cannot work in the presence of lead, thus requiring a continued use of lead-free gasoline and engines that can use it. In the longer run, the removal of lead from gasoline may be seen as a means of reducing other pollutants from the gasoline engine, rather than an end in itself.

The extent of pollution from gasoline and diesel engines is largely a factor of design. It is not clear what damage is caused by the emission of nitrogen oxides, except in combination with other gaseous pollutants. It is clear, however, that carbon monoxide is undesirable, as are the hydrocarbons. Hydrocarbons are emitted from both the crankcase and the engine exhaust. Reburning of crankcase gases has been demonstrated as a means of reducing total hydrocarbon emission. Similarly, carbon monoxide in the exhaust can be treated by either absorption or catalytic oxidation.

In addition to these forms of pollution, two other forms exist: odor and dust. As was just noted, diesel engines are the worst offenders in terms of odor. Research is in progress to identify the sources of odor and possible means of control. Dust is generated from two sources: wear of the parts comprising the motive-power unit of a vehicle; and wear between wheel and bearing surface. The former of these is probably relatively insignificant. However, the dust produced by friction between rubber tires and asphalt, concrete, or bitumen pavement surfaces is considerable. Some dust is also produced from friction between steel wheel and steel rail, but this is generally less than that from road vehicles. In Chicago, settled dust from roads and alleys comprises about 30% of all settled dust, while that from railroads is less than 5%.[26]

The extent of pollution from a new facility is clearly dependent largely on vehicle designs and fuel types used, neither of which is specifically the concern of the transportation planner, although an understanding of how they arise is an essential component of responsive planning. The effect of vehicle pollution on the surrounding environment will be determined by the vehicle types, the amount of traffic, and the prevailing climatic conditions. Basically, natural processes can deal remarkably well with even relatively high concentrations of man-made and natural pollution. Winds and general air currents will usually disperse and dilute pollution, and rain and lightning will cause the pollutants to be returned to the earth, where other natural processes utilize the products. Problems of pollution occur largely from two causes: production of pollutants greater than natural processes can handle; and accumulation of air pollutants due to atmospheric conditions in inversion and separation.[27] The second of these causes is often also due to the effects of man on his environment. The likelihood of pollution will clearly be related to some extent to the location of a facility. If a facility is located in a river valley that is a frequent site for temperature inversions, then serious local air pollution is likely to be generated. Similarly, the location in relation to wind direction and velocity and other existing pollutants will affect the potential seriousness of pollution. Thus, a facility located to the west of a metropolitan area where winds are largely from the west will contribute to the existing pollution of the metropolitan area. If the facility were to the east, it is likely that its pollution would be diluted and dispersed away from the metropolitan area.

The final major type of environmental impact that is considered is that of visual intrusion. In order to determine what constitutes visual intrusion, the physical design of the facility will have to be examined. If the facility is built in bored or cut-and-cover tunnel, it clearly is not seen and, therefore, cannot intrude, except insofar as ventilation, station, or interchange facilities may require external construction of some form. Similarly, a facility constructed in cuttings or retained structure below grade will have minimal intrusion on the landscape, no matter what the details are of the specific design of the facility. For instance, an expressway depressed far enough to permit overbridges that do not alter the level of the existing streets will not be visible, apart from fences and tops of lamp standards, from further than about one hundred yards from the top edge of the cutting or retaining wall.

A facility at grade or elevated will obviously be able to be seen from some distance away. Whether or not it is considered to be an intrusion will depend upon several factors. Among these will be the type of construction used, and the surrounding objects. A facility built on twenty-foot high concrete columns and constructed through woodland on the side of a hill will clearly stand out and be at variance with its surroundings. The same facility constructed in a downtown area among steel, concrete, and glass buildings will blend with its surroundings much more easily, and may well be considered nonintrusive.

From these considerations, a possible basis for definition of visual intrusion can be built. Two basic concepts emerge: the facility has to be visible; and it has to be "at variance" with its setting. These two concepts may form a basic definition of visual intrusion. This is by no means an exhaustive or complete definition, and it is clearly necessary to extend the definition of the facility to include all its appurtenances, such as lighting columns, road signs, fences, ramps, signal lights, etc. Visual intrusion, unlike noise and air pollution, is entirely a facility-design dependent impact. Hence, total control and elimination of visual intrusion can be attained by careful facility design and planning, particularly when carried out conjointly with planning and design of nearby buildings.

Impact Attenuation

Having identified briefly each of the basic environmental impacts of a transportation facility, attention can now be turned to methods of control or elimination of these impacts. Earlier discussions in this section on air pollution suggest that this impact is the least tractable one to control or eliminate from the facility-planning viewpoint. The only influence that can be exerted concerns the overall choice of location, and this will usually be predicated on the grounds of facility service and use, with little or no flexibility in terms of the impact of air pollution. One situation does exist in which planning and design of the facility is much more concerned with pollution. This is the case where a facility is to be tunnelled, and ventilation has to be provided. In such an instance, the design of the ventilation system can incorporate means to reduce some of the more harmful products of the vehicles and considerable care needs to be taken in the siting of ventilator outlets. One other aspect over which control can be exercised is the production of dust. Here it is necessary to determine the relative merits of various types of track and maintenance procedures on the same criterion.

Thus, given that the planner has little possibility of ameliorating the generation of air pollution by a transportation facility, he should nevertheless be very well aware of the consequences of a facility in producing air pollution. There is a need to determine the levels of pollution generated by differing facilities and the climatic conditions that will affect the dispersion, dilution, and direction of the pollution. The consequences of air pollution need also to be known in terms of the effects on the ecology of the areas surrounding the facility and the likely effects on human population. Given a knowledge of such consequences, location of the transportation facility should be determined in such a way as to attempt to minimize these adverse effects, subject to other locational constraints.

The various ecological impacts fall basically into two categories. First are those impacts that will occur regardless of the specific location of the facility, although their magnitude may vary from one location to another. These will include the effects of air and water pollution on plants and animals, the reduction in vegetation, and certain changes in the drainage patterns. The extent of these impacts may possibly determine whether or not the facility should even be constructed. This observation is clearly also true for a number of the other impacts that have been discussed.

In terms of the other ecological impacts, a trained ecologist is needed to indicate some of the necessary strategies to eliminate or reduce the impacts. Several of these will be both design and location features.

Noise and visual intrusion can usefully be considered together. Visual intrusion is governed entirely by the design process; noise propagation from the facility is also governed largely by design. There are five basic design forms available for a transportation facility that is not placed in a tunnel: depressed in open cut, depressed between retaining walls, at grade, elevated on fill (sloped or retained walls), and elevated on structure (see Figure 6-1).[28,29] Noise can be considered as radiating equally in all directions from the vehicles on the facility. Its propagation properties can be changed in two ways: sound can be absorbed by the surfaces around the facility, or barriers can be erected to deflect the sound. These barriers may be part of the facility construction or may be specified building construction on either side of the facility.[30] Basically, a depressed facility will incorporate some structure within it that is capable of deflecting sound waves. A sloped cutting will deflect according to the angle of slope. Simple geometry will indicate the effects of this (see Figure 6-2). For instance, a cutting sloped at 30 degrees to the horizontal on either side of a 130-foot roadway width will deflect sounds such that, if the roadway is 20 feet below ground level and the height of the exhaust of a truck is 15 feet above the roadway surface, a house 20 feet high which is 700 feet away will not be affected by direct sounds. Similarly, even from the second floor windows, none of the roadway surface would be visible, and in fact all that would be seen would be the top 4 feet of the cutting on the farthest side. An increase of the side slope to 45 degrees would still only permit the house to be 600 feet away for no audible or visual perception of the facility. However, if the facility is depressed between vertical retaining walls, the house can still only be moved 80 feet nearer, to 520 feet away. The construction of a sound-reflecting parapet along either the top of a cutting or the top of the retaining wall can make considerable gains. If such a parapet were 5 feet high, a 30-degree slope would permit buildings within 340 feet, a 45-degree slope—300 feet, and vertical retaining walls—250 feet. In such a case, however, a form of visual intrusion with a 5-foot high parapet along the length of the facility has been added. Elevated facilities are a much greater concern. Visually they may be constructed in such a way as to fit in with their environment. Sloped, grassed embankments

131

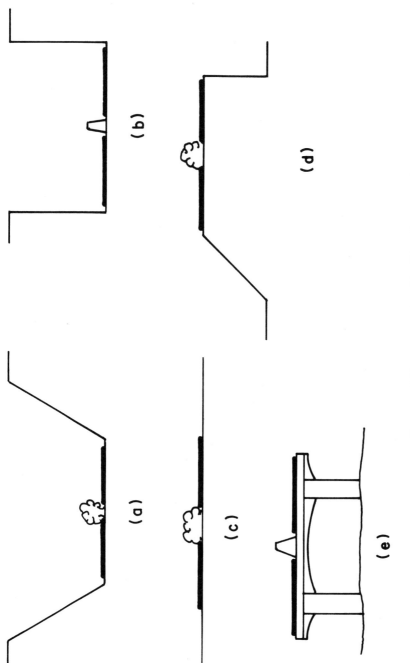

Figure 6-1. Forms of Transportation Facility Construction.

132

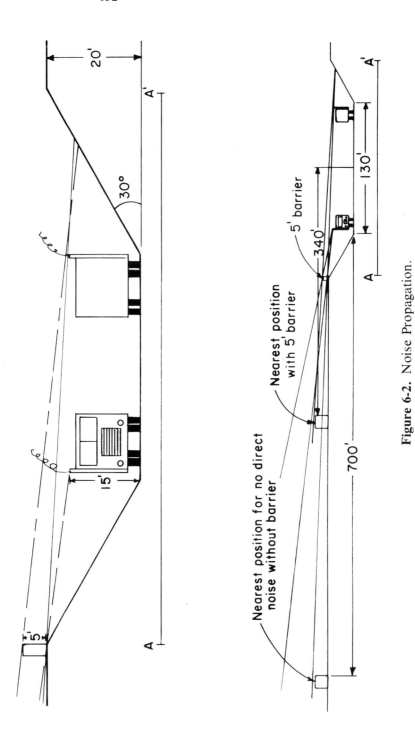

Figure 6-2. Noise Propagation.

with tree and hedge planting along them can permit a facility to blend relatively well into a rural landscape. Other concomitant benefits of these features are increased sound and pollution absorption. Attention to the design of the facility in terms of alignment can also serve to help here.

It is not difficult to continue to extend examples of the effects of facility design on visual and noise impacts. It should be clear from this cursory glance at the problems that much can be done to reduce the visual and audible impacts of transportation facilities by careful design. The precise ways in which design should be carried out will also require some detailed knowledge of the more precise measurements of noise and a careful evaluation of visual aspects.

Energy-Flow Theory: Potential Solution to the Problem of Impact Measurement

This chapter has illustrated, particularly in the sections on social and environmental impacts, how complex an issue it is to identify a metric that can be applied to all impact categories. Such a common metric would obviously facilitate the evaluation of the absolute magnitude and the relative significance of different types of impacts and, also, even more importantly, would permit the development of a universally applicable analysis technique.

The relatively recent development of an energy-flow methodology due to Odum and his associates,[31] could potentially provide such a metric and analysis technique. Developed in the context of ecological impact measurement and assessment, recent research efforts have attempted to offer insight into the suitability and applicability of this impact-assessment approach to the transportation sector.[32]

The basic rationale underlying the energy-flow methodology is that all mental and physical processes can be considered in terms of energy flow. The use of energy principles (First and Second Laws of Thermodynamics, and the Maximum Power Principle) allows economic and environmental processes to be expressed in common terms. Flows and storage of different forms of energy can be measured in terms of heat equivalents (calories), irrespective of the context in which energy flow and storage occur.

In principle, the energy-flow or energy-accounting methodology is applicable to impact identification, measurement, and analysis in the transportation sector. Serious problems still remain concerning the data requirements and effort involved in applying the methodology to large-scale transportation-impact evaluations. Greater research efforts are still required to prove the suitability of the approach for the transportation planner and designer.

Concluding Remarks

This chapter has attempted to put together at least a cursory review of the problems and methods of identification and assessment of the impacts or consequences of the provision of transportation facilities. It would probably require a separate lengthy book even to begin to cover the subject in any depth. However, the intention here has been to generate an awareness of the range, types, and complexity of problems that exist in the evaluation of impacts of transportation on nonusers. One specific problem, perhaps the most important one of all, has not been considered in these topics so far. This is the problem of scaling.

On numerous occasions it was stated, after considering a specific impact, that the effects of this impact from the provision of a facility must be taken into account in planning the facility. However, planning, as it is discussed here, is a "rational" process. This implies that, if a number of criteria are generated that must operate on the planning process, some means must exist for interpreting significant values of the criteria and summing their combined consequences. This presents a number of problems in terms of value judgments of impacts and consequences.

Current planning techniques tend to infer "values" for these criteria (if they are considered) on the basis of the response of people affected. This generates a weighting process that is related to the articulateness of various community groups and their political power. This is not necessarily an unacceptable solution, but there is a feeling that it is a suboptimal solution, since articulate, politically powerful groups may not necessarily be aware of some consequences or of the importance of some consequences. Hence, the analyst attempts to generate optimal solutions that presume an absolute scaling of criteria. At this point in time, no real progress has been made to set up scaling of this type. Before it can be done, it is probably necessary to obtain a deeper understanding of the nature, extent, and perception of these various impacts.

7

Cost-Effectiveness

The Need for An Alternative Evaluation Technique

In chapter 6 a variety of impacts are identified and discussed, whose measurement, analysis, and interpretation have caused major concerns and problems for the transportation-systems analyst. These impacts are those which are difficult, if not impossible, to quantify or express in monetary terms. This chapter concentrates on the discussion of an evaluation technique, namely cost-effectiveness analysis, which is thought to be applicable when dealing with nonquantifiable impacts or impacts that are subject to ordinal classification only.

Discussions in the previous chapters outlined a number of drawbacks to conventional methods of evaluation of transportation alternatives. These drawbacks are related to their ability or inability to deal with the concepts of *efficiency* and *effectiveness*. The concept of efficiency is concerned with obtaining one's "money's worth" from an alternative. In other words, it is concerned with obtaining on an investment returns that are worthwhile. In general, the three conventional techniques of evaluation—net present worth, benefit/cost ratios and rate of return—are all concerned with measuring the efficiency of alternatives.

These schemes, or techniques, for measuring efficiency require, by their nature, that all items for consideration are reduced to a common metric, which is generally a monetary unit, e.g., the dollar. This means that efficiency is measured simply in terms of the monetary efficiency of alternatives and is concerned with those items of costs and benefits that can be reduced to a common metric. This leads to a very narrow set of consequences being considered and is liable, in turn, to yield decisions that are seriously suboptimal in terms of the urban or regional system.

The concept of effectiveness stems from the application of a systems analysis framework to the formulation and evaluation of alternative solutions for transportation problems.[1] In the systems-analysis framework, goals and objectives are initially determined and are used to generate alternatives. The extent to which a plan, or proposal, attains the objectives is a measure of its effectiveness. Since it is frequently the case that the alternatives generated will attain different levels of objective fulfillment, it is appropriate to assess alternatives, not only in terms of efficiency, but

135

also in terms of effectiveness. The strategy of cost-effectiveness analysis is an attempt to represent, in a decision-oriented framework, the relative efficiency and effectiveness of a set of alternative strategies.

Weighting Effectiveness

The judgement of alternative strategies by examining effectiveness implies a ranking and weighting of the objectives and extent of objective attainment.[2] This immediately raises the problem of who is to determine the weights and ranking of alternatives. A number of possibilities can be entertained here. Among those who may be considered are: The engineers and planners involved in the study, elected officials of the region considered, independent planning consultants, state or federal agencies concerned with the project, or a panel of experts appointed by the elected officials. Other alternatives are obviously possible. Clearly the weights arrived at through this process will be subjective and, being subjective, will almost certainly be strongly biased. Although it may well be desirable that the weighting should be carried out on a subjective basis, it is not easy to determine what subjective biases will lead to good decision making.

It may appear to be desirable to assemble a panel of experts to assess various areas of objective attainment as an input to the decision-making process. For instance, an architect may examine the visual aesthetics of the proposals, psychologists and sociologists may deal with human consequences, and economists with regional development and growth consequences. Considerable problems arise still in the process of weighting these various viewpoints, and determining a good decision.

Particular problems arise when two objectives are, to some extent, in conflict. It then becomes necessary to have information on the difference in importance between two such objectives. This type of situation is examined in the following paragraphs.

Suppose a plan is to be developed for affording greater accessibility of suburban areas to the central business district (CBD) of a city and for reducing the amount of auto exhaust pollution in the city. Further, it is assumed that a mass-transportation system is not available, and that the accessibility must be provided by highways. Clearly, the objectives are likely to be in conflict. A representation of the goal achievement of four alternatives may be represented as shown in Figure 7-1.[3] Clearly, if decreasing air pollution is of overriding importance, then alternative 4 is the best choice. Likewise, if increased accessibility is of paramount importance, alternative 1 is the best alternative. However, if neither of these situations are appropriate, the choice is not specified by the assessment and specifi-

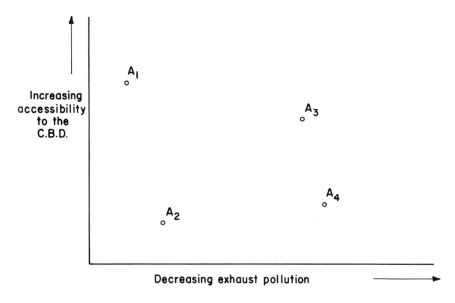

Figure 7-1. Example of Conflicting Objectives.

cation of consequences in terms of these two objectives. If, however, a rank order of desirability of the objectives, together with a specific weighting, can be obtained, a decision can be made between the above alternatives. For instance, suppose decreasing air pollution is twice as desirable as increasing CBD accessibility. In this case, indifference curves between the two objectives can be constructed. These indifference curves represent combinations of the two objectives with the same combined value. The value can be written as in equation (7.1).

$$V = 2(Obj)_1 + (Obj)_2 \qquad (7.1)$$

where $(Obj)_1$ = the reduction of air pollution

$(Obj)_2$ = the increase of CBD accessibility

These indifference curves are shown in Figure 7-2. It is clear from this figure that alternative 3 is the best alternative, since it yields the highest combined value, while being neither the best in attaining Objective 1, nor the best in attaining Objective 2.

Several problems arise in the determination of weights such as those used in the above example. First, the problem again exists of who it is that should establish the weights. Many of the problems arising in relation to this were already discussed. At the present time, a change in the make-up of the group responsible for determining the subjective weights can be ob-

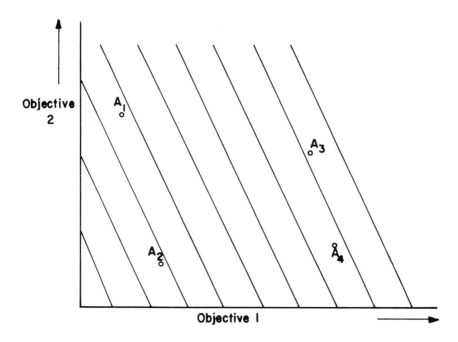

Figure 7-2. Indifference Curves Relating to Two Objectives.

served. For some time, in transportation evaluation, the weights have largely been determined by engineers and planners, modified by the elected regional representatives. Now, the establishment of weights is moving further towards the communities involved in the discussion of consequences of alternative plans. It is clear, from past experience, that decisions made by the analyst alone are not generally the best when viewed for a region as a whole. The present trends toward community participation in the weighting procedures is a welcome move, and should lead eventually to new mechanisms of establishing weights.

A second problem associated with weighting procedures concerns the mechanism for obtaining information from people on the trade-offs between objectives. Basically, the information should be obtainable by survey techniques. However, obtaining information on attitudes and opinions is fraught with problems. Such surveys rely on the rationality of human judgment and the ability of people to form reliable judgements of abstract concepts and ideas. In particular, opinions and attitudes to currently nonexistent alternatives are rarely reliable guides to values pertinent when such alternatives exist. Furthermore, opinions and attitudes are highly dependent upon current and past experience.

In surveying people to determine their opinions, the weighting procedure necessitates the development of aggregated opinions and attitudes. It is not clear whether each individual's opinion should have equal weight to any other individual, or some individuals should have greater weights assigned to their opinions. There are also possibilities of attempting to determine the intensity of feelings associated with certain opinions and attitudes.

The use of theories and techniques from applied psychology, particularly for determining stable attitudes, as opposed to transitory opinions, appears to have considerable promise in this area.[4] These theories and techniques, however, still leave unanswered the questions about the best method of aggregating the attitudes of numerous individuals.

The Cost-Effectiveness Method

The cost-effectiveness method is a way of assessing, simultaneously, both the efficiency and effectiveness of a set of alternatives. In essence, the method gives a formal framework to the usual decision-making process, in which the decision maker takes the outputs of an evaluation process and weights this against the intangible or irreducible consequences of the alternatives.

The cost-effectiveness method was first developed in the military context[5] where goal attainment frequently cannot be quantified, but where the relationship between cost and effectiveness, for example, of alternative weapon systems can be ranked. This would allow the military decision maker to choose that alternative that might have the lowest cost for rendering a specific desirable destructive effect. Or, he might choose that alternative weapon system that can achieve the greatest military gains for a fixed predetermined budget.

The technique involves the use of two sets of measures to indicate efficiency and effectiveness: costs and indicators of objective attainment. The choice of alternative is made on the basis of these two sets of measures, thereby eliminating the need for reducing all the attributes or consequences to a single metric.

Costs

For the cost-effectiveness technique, costs are defined as the total monetary outlays needed in order to achieve, or obtain, the alternative in question. This assumes that the price mechanism operates in such a way that the resources expended on each alternative are accurately valued by the monetary unit being used (e.g., the dollar). In the event that there are strong grounds for supposing that the price mechanism does not operate in this way, then costs may be measured in some other, more suitable, units. Various cost models may be used to determine the costs of a set of alternatives. The specific cost model deemed most appropriate for a particular scheme should clearly be used. It should be noted that the evaluation techniques discussed in chapter 5 have a single cost model alone. Clearly, an advantage of the cost-effectiveness technique is the fact that it permits the use of any appropriate cost model.

The conventional evaluation techniques use a cost model that may be itemized as follows:

1. Traveled-way structural costs
2. Right-of-way acquisition costs
3. Terminal-facility costs
4. Mobile-components costs

Such a cost model is based upon a consideration of the physical components of the system, and the outlays required for each component. The common breakdown of costs used by industry is:

1. Research and development costs
2. Capital investments or fixed facility costs
3. Variable or operating costs

Yet another possible cost model might comprise:

1. Research and development costs
2. Construction costs
3. Financing costs
4. Operating costs
5. Maintenance costs
6. Management costs

All of these cost models are valid, and any one may be the most suitable in a particular instance. It may possibly be that several cost models should be used in a particular instance. For instance, yet another cost model would evaluate the marginal costs of offering various types of services. In particular, such a model would give information concerning the marginal costs of providing an additional transit link, or an additional freeway interchange, etc. It would clearly give information particularly pertinent to the determination of the trade-offs between alternatives. Costs may also be modeled on a time-dependent basis, with information supplied of the costs, at various points in time, as a function of construction phasing or scheduled operations of the transportation plan.

Whatever cost model is used, a considerable advantage is obtained if the costs are placed in a framework in which they are related to objective attainment. Thus, specific alternatives are designed to achieve certain objectives. Understanding of the alternatives by decision makers will be considerably aided by the apportionment of total program costs to the attainment of particular objectives. Thus, for instance, costs for a transportation system may be apportioned as:

1. Route miles of service—dollars per mile
2. Seat miles of service—dollars per mile
3. Passenger miles of service—dollars per passenger mile and so forth

Discounting the costs over a planning period would clearly be appropriate in assessing the cost for various alternatives. As for the conventional evaluation techniques, it is obviously necessary to take into account the times at which various costs will be encountered. Also, as was indicated in earlier discussions, conditions of uncertainty should desirably be taken into account. Research into the application of such methods as Bayesian statistics[6] to the determination of the uncertainty of various costs being encountered over time would be advantageous.

Effectiveness

Effectiveness has already been defined as the degree to which objectives are attained. The framework of the technique of cost-effectiveness is sufficiently broad and flexible that effectiveness may simply be defined as the characterization of all the relevant consequences of the alternatives exclusive of costs.[7]

In relatively simple problems, such as those encountered in evaluating many military systems,[8] it may be possible to assess goal achievement on the basis of a few quantitative measures, which can be combined to yield a mathematical model.[9] Such a mathematical model can then be used with the appropriate cost model(s) to yield a recommended alternative. In general, the problems facing the transportation planner are less simple, and many of the consequences may be unquantifiable.

In most cases, a quantitative model of effectiveness cannot, therefore, be developed. If a subjective ranking scheme is used, such as that described above, much information may be obscured and too many subjective choices are left to the analyst. In using the cost-effectiveness approach, goal achievement may be described mathematically, verbally or pictorially, and the decision maker is enabled to construct a composite picture of the consequences of each alternative.

This procedure is very similar to the individual's decision-making process. For instance, the individual who chooses a car goes through much the same procedure. Having decided that he wishes to buy a new car, he has a wide range of makes and models from which to choose. On the basis of various pieces of information from salesmen, dealers, advertisements, technical documents, friends, and perhaps consumer ratings, he obtains an image of the effectiveness of each alternative that will enable him to narrow down his choice to, perhaps, two or three alternatives. Certain alternatives may be rejected out of hand because of cost (where this exceeds the allowable budget) and others will be rejected on the assessment of their effectiveness for the purposes for which the car is wanted. The final choice among the eventual two or three alternatives will be made, possibly, on such bases as the availability of particular colors, the opinion of a close friend, or some other such criteria. This final decision determines the "worth" of the effectiveness of the chosen alternative and is an entirely subjective decision. This situation is very closely analogous to the use of cost-effectiveness in decisions in transportation.

The cost-effectiveness framework requires the description of the consequences that will stem from any alternative. It does not, however, restrict the ways in which these consequences are to be described. There is no attempt to oversimplify the evaluation process, nor to "force concentration on the strictly measurable consequences of alternative plans."[10] In arriving at the descriptions of consequences, it may be advantageous to structure consequences into categories. Such categories might include the following:

1. Consequences of inputs:
   a. Opportunities lost due to resource commitments.
   b. Changes in employment.
   c. Changes in real income.
   d. Scarcities of material resources.
   e. Promotion of previously unused resources.
   f. Social disruption due to purchase of right-of-way.
   g. Modifications of human activity patterns and resource allocations due to the taking of land parcels.
   h. Others.
2. Consequences of performance outputs:
   a. Changes in community growth patterns.
   b. Changes in market areas and competitive positions of various activities.
   c. Social unification due to increased accessibility.
   d. Expanded social, economic, and cultural realms of people due to increased accessibility.
   e. Modifications of human activity patterns and resource allocations due to changes in accessibility.
   f. Changes in the prices of public and private goods due to changes in accessibility.
   g. Changes in employment patterns due to changes in accessibility.

h. Lives and resources saved or lost due to changes in transportation safety.

i. Others.

3. Consequences of concomitant outputs:

a. Social and psychological effects of creation or destruction of physical barriers by transportation facilities.

b. Aesthetic impacts of facilities.

c. Changes in crime rate created by transportation structures.

d. Physiological effects of air pollution due to transportation.

e. Psychological and physiological impacts of sound and light emitted by transportation vehicles and facilities.

f. Effects of changes in the safety properties of the interface between transportation facilities and their environments.

g. Modifications of human activity patterns and resource allocations because of changes in site characteristics due to concomitant outputs.

h. Others.[11]

As sophistication in the application of the technique is developed, the selection and breakdown of consequences will inevitably be developed into a more rigorous framework. The choice of the consequences to be used is clearly of some importance. Two criteria may be used to help determine the consequences to be considered. These criteria are feasibility and relevance. Thomas and Schofer[12] give an excellent diagrammatic indication of the effect of feasibility on the decision making process. Essentially, feasibility refers to the level of detail of the knowledge supplied about various consequences and the number of consequences to be considered. In brief terms, as the level of complexity (number of consequences, level of detail) increases, there comes a point where the quality of the decision is no longer increased. Furthermore, as complexity increases, the associated costs of supplying the information increase, while the ease of making a decision decreases rapidly. The four diagrams of Figure 7-3[13] illustrate this very clearly. The point to be made by these diagrams is that the net quality of the decision making clearly has an optimum in terms of level of detail and number of factors considered. At the present time, however, it appears likely that information for decision making is well to the left of that optimum. Nevertheless, for many evaluation situations, it would be advisable to bear this criterion in mind and ensure that the number of factors and their level of detail are within the bounds of feasibility.

The second criterion is that of relevancy. There are several parameters associated with relevancy. First, it is important that there is an understanding of the transportation system and its relationship to the environment. Without such understanding, it will be difficult to determine the relevance of various factors. Relevancy will be determined by the relationship between a consequence and the objectives of the planning proc-

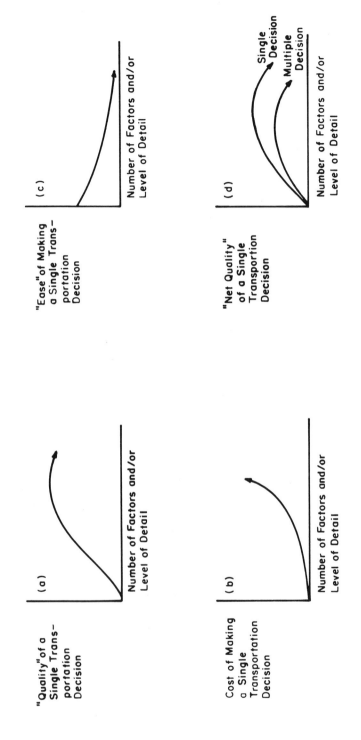

Figure 7-3. The Criterion of Feasibility in Selecting Effectiveness Data.

ess. Given that the objectives have been completely formulated, a consequence that has no relevance to the stated objectives is not relevant to the decision-making process. Similarly, if a consequence is identical for all alternatives, or is, in some other way, unable to affect the decisions between the alternatives, it is not relevant.

Concluding Remarks

There is clearly much more that could be dealt with in relation to the various procedures inherent within the cost-effectiveness framework. However, space constraints do not allow their consideration in this book. There are clearly numerous cost models that can be developed for use in the cost-effectiveness framework. There is also considerable scope for research into the measures of effectiveness. The factors to be included among the measures of effectiveness have been discussed in chapter 6.

It is clear that the cost-effectiveness framework is potentially able to assist the decision maker to make better decisions than the more conventional evaluation techniques.[14] It is also clear, however, that the efficacy of the technique is highly dependent upon the formation of a complete spectrum of goals and the development of pertinent objectives. The cost-effectiveness framework can never be better than the goal formulation procedure that precedes it.

An Example

To illustrate a potential application of the cost-effectiveness method to transportation problems, a recent freeway-location study is used. The purpose of the study was to determine a preferred routing for a circumferential freeway to a major urban area. The study was undertaken in 1969-1970 and utilized the procedures outlined in PPM 20-8.[15] Initially, a freeway corridor was defined, measuring approximately four miles wide and sixty-five miles long. Within this corridor, it was intended to locate the route for a freeway that would generally require a right-of-way of 300 feet or less in width. The primary portion of the corridor, within which most freedom for the selection of a route existed, covered a distance of about 30 miles, from the intersection of one planned radial freeway in the north to the intersection with an existing radial freeway in the southwest of the corridor.

The initial task of the study was to define a series of "mini-corridors," each one of about one-quarter of a mile in width, within which a potential freeway route would exist. The use of mini-corridors served two purposes. First, they are small enough to permit reasonably accurate cost estimates to be developed for a freeway, since the number of structures, form of construction, and number and type of interchanges can be estimated accurately enough for preliminary cost estimating. Second, the mini-corridors are too broad to allow any identification of specific parcels of land that would be required for construction, thus preventing premature property sales, panics, and so forth.

A total of nine mini-corridors were located in the primary freeway corridor. These individual mini-corridors crossed and overlapped each other at certain points within the corridor. As a result, it was possible to define thirty-one potential freeway routes that used various segments of the mini-corridors. These thirty-one routes were next subjected to a detailed cost-effectiveness analysis, with the effectiveness measures defined by PPM 20-8.[16] Many of the effectiveness measures are assessed for the probable line of the freeway itself—for example, safety, impact on public utilities, and noise relate to a specific route through a combination of mini-corridor segments. Certain other measures, e.g., economic activity, employment, disruption of school districts, conduct and financing of local government, and operation of other transportation facilities, can only be assessed by considering entire communities that border on or include portions of a selected route. Thus, these consequences or impacts are not those occurring solely in the probable path of the freeway, but are those that would occur in the communities adjacent to or including the freeway.

Numerical estimates were made of the cost, length, number of parcels of land required, number of interchanges and number of structures (principally bridges) required for each of the thirty-one alternative routes. For the remaining measures of effectiveness or impact, subjective estimates were made on whether the freeway route would have a positive, negative, or neutral effect on each measure. The result of this process is shown in Figure 7-4.

A number of important points can be made about Figure 7-4, all of which serve to demonstrate the properties of cost-effectiveness as a method of evaluation. It is clear that the decision maker is presented with all of the information that is available for an evaluation. Apart from the necessity to make subjective estimates of the actual direction of the various consequences, there are no implicit values or judgments in the process. If the decision maker wishes to value the number of parcels of land to be acquired as the only criterion of effectiveness, he may do so. Figure 7-5 shows a graphical representation of the trade-off that results. Depending upon the value that the decision maker wishes to place on a parcel of land, his decision would be to select one of routes 15 or 31. Route 15 implies the highest value of a parcel and 31 the lowest.

For a more complex analysis, the decision maker may take into ac-

147

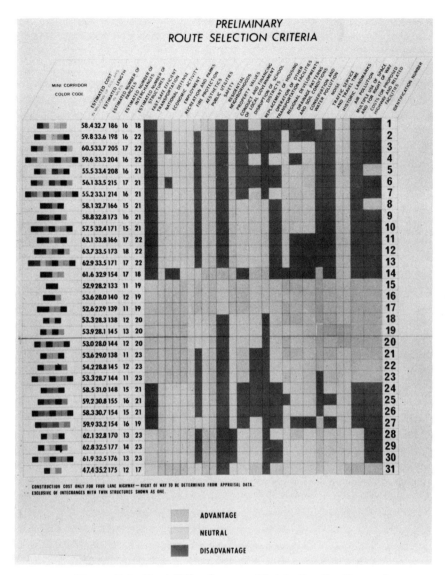

Figure 7-4. Cost-Effectiveness Matrix for the Example.

count all of the consequences listed. If all are given an equal weight, the preferred alternative, on the basis of effectiveness, will be route 15. This route gives no negative impacts, and produces twelve positive impacts. Alternative 17 yields eleven positive impacts and no negative ones and costs $52.6 million, while route 15 costs $52.9 million. If the decision maker

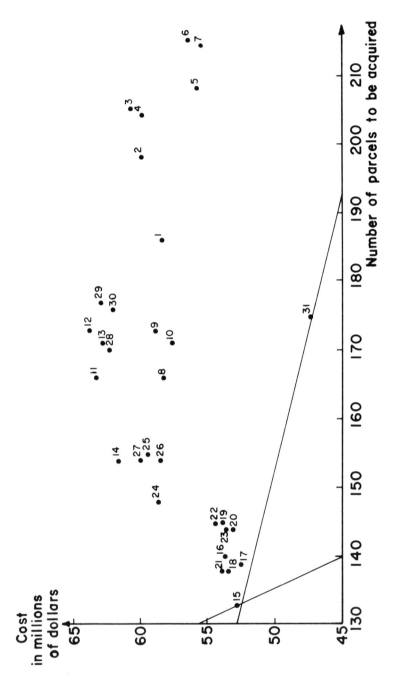

Figure 7-5. Trade-off between Cost and Number of Parcels of Land Required.

considers that one extra positive impact is worth at least $300,000, he will still opt for route 15. This is reinforced further if he considers the number of parcels of land to be acquired, where six more are required for 17 than for 15. On the other hand, route 31 gives eleven positive impacts and two negative ones, costs only $47.4 million, but requires 175 parcels of land, which is 42 more than for alternative 15. Clearly, the decision maker has freedom to trade off various consequences of the alternative routes, in order to select the desired route.

Thus, the cost-effectiveness approach is very transparent, allowing the decision maker extensive freedom to select weights and to use or ignore information about impacts. The information presented does not require the decision maker to have extensive technical skills in transportation planning or any other area.

The example also serves to illustrate some of the problems and shortcomings of the approach. It is difficult, for example, to assimilate information on twenty-eight criteria or measures of effectiveness for thirty-one alternatives. Second, it becomes clear that the amount or size of an impact may be very relevant to the evaluation, while this information is generally not provided by the present state of the art. For example, the differences between routes 15, 16, and 17 are only one or two positive impacts and $1 million, where this latter represents less than 2% of the cost of any alternative. Clearly, if the positive impacts differ substantially in size, though not in direction, among these three alternatives, then it is quite conceivable that route 16 or route 17 would be the preferred one and not 15. Thus, it is clear that there is need for considerable further research on the cost-effectiveness procedure, while the procedure shows considerable promise as an improved evaluation mechanism in transportation planning.

8

Summary and Conclusions

Review of Evaluation Techniques

In the preceding chapters, an outline has been given of two basic approaches to the evaluation of transportation systems. First, the more traditional economic-evaluation procedures were described. These procedures mandate the inclusion in the evaluation process of only those costs and benefits that can be monetized. A number of controversial issues were uncovered in considering economic evaluation techniques. These issues included the question of the appropriateness of including consumer surplus in the analysis, the treatment of the temporal nature of transportation investment, the selection of a method for calculating the trade-off between costs and benefits, and the valuation of travel-time savings, accidents, and other nonmonetary costs and benefits.

In general, the economic-evaluation procedures involve a strict accounting of costs and benefits over the life of each alternative investment option or policy. As such, they provide the decision maker with a single numeric value for each option, thus permitting a rapid, unidimensional assessment of each option. Each of the procedures requires the estimation of a set of forecasts of travel volumes, operating costs, and initial capital costs, together with such data as numbers of fatal accidents, maintenance costs, and policing costs. Given these inputs, the determination of project life and the selection of one or more discount rates, a net present worth, benefit/cost ratio, or rate of return can be computed. With current high-speed computers and interactive programming techniques, the decision maker can be provided with a variety of evaluative data points, wherein the assumptions for each alternative may be varied over a range of feasible values and the sensitivity of the numeric outputs determined.

The second approach is termed a cost-effectiveness evaluation and was developed initially for application in military decision making. The technique attempts to circumvent the strong quantitative orientation of the more traditional economic evaluation and allows the consideration of a much broader set of consequences of transportation plans and policies. In addition to broadening the set of consequences, the cost-effectiveness procedure also opens up the possibility of considering the consequences to a broader group of people. Indeed, the technique is well able, in concept, to handle the evaluation of the consequences to both users and non-users.

151

The technique is grounded in the systems-analytic framework, wherein the definition of goals and objectives permits the development of a concept of effectiveness. The cost-effectiveness procedure is, thus, a framework within which the decision maker can assess the various levels of achievement of objectives that may be obtained at various levels of cost. This enables the decision maker to enter political and societal values to determine preferred plans and policies from the evaluation process. Potentially, the cost-effectiveness process permits the consideration of the full set of consequences of any policy or plan, regardless of who may experience the consequences. The limitation in the method to do this resides in the completeness of the goal-setting process and is not a function of the technique itself.

Third, one may consider impact analysis as either an element of the cost-effectiveness approach or as a method in its own right. As an element of the cost-effectiveness approach, it represents the enumeration of the measures of effectiveness. Thus, one may use the number of residences and businesses to be relocated, the level of noise and air pollution generated, the extent of likely land-use changes, etc. as measures of effectiveness to compare construction with enlargement. Likewise, many of the same measures can be used to assess nonconstruction policies, such as an area-licensing scheme, the introduction of fares-free mass transit, and the installation of an area traffic control system.

Alternatively, impact may be more loosely structured to form an ad hoc evaluation procedure. The preparation of environmental impact statements, and the development of the broader preconstruction hearing process in highway construction,[1] represents the use of impact analysis as an evaluative mechanism. In theory, the public is offered impact information and the values or weights appropriate to this information are inferred from the levels of public reaction. A strict cost-effectiveness approach is not involved in this procedure.

Finally, there has been some recent resurgence of interest in the idea of "value-capture policies".[2] This procedure is not discussed in detail in the earlier parts of this book because the authors do not consider it to be a realistic evaluation procedure, nor a policy that can be implemented. Nevertheless, recent interest in it requires that some mention be made of it. The method is based upon the observation that most transportation improvements generate accessibility improvements that, in turn, cause increases in property values. The argument then suggests that projects may be selected upon the basis of those that generate the maximum value increase per unit of project cost. Second, it is suggested that government should finance the project construction by taxing the value increase so that it returns to the original cause of the value increase, rather than accruing to the property owners who benefit.

On the surface, this appears to be a reasonable procedure, both for project selection and project financing. However, there is a serious flaw in the argument that is discussed in chapter 1. For all value increases generated by any public facility improvement, one can usually find an equal set of value decreases. For example, a new expressway between city A and city B may generate increased land values surrounding each interchange. But the arterial that it replaces may pass through village X, village Y, and village Z. While the loss of traffic on the arterial may benefit some of the properties along that route, the loss of business in the villages will most probably far outweigh these improvements. Similarly, there may be serious losses in land value between interchanges, where pockets of farmland may be rendered uneconomical. Similarly, it has already been pointed out that reductions in accidents by facility improvements also bring reductions in the income of doctors, hospitals, auto repairers, and undertakers who would be needed to take care of the results of the accidents.

One may, in fact, propose a corollary to Newton's Third Law of Motion,[3] which states that for every action there is an equal and opposite reaction. The corollary would be that *for every value increase caused by the improvement of a public facility (e.g., a highway), there will be an equal value decrease experienced by some other element of society.* Thus, a value-capture policy could lead to suits to recover value lost due to a facility improvement that would equal the value apparently gained by that facility. Since such suits would probably seek damages above and beyond the strict value change, and since court costs would also be involved, the government agency will end up with no finances for the improvement, but a loss beyond any value captured. Likewise, the use of the procedures for project selection is infeasible. Clearly, the arguments put forward here state that there can be no net value added by any facility, and, therefore, there can be no comparison between projects that would allow selection of one over another through this process.

A Critique of Economic-Evaluation and Cost-Effectiveness Methods

Economic Evaluation

There are two inherent faults in the economic-evaluation process. First, it is restricted to dealing with only those costs and benefits that can be given "monetary" values, such as time, accidents, and vehicle-operating costs. While one may defend this by stating that only those costs and benefits that have monetary value, as shown by a willingness to trade them for other items of value, should enter the evaluation scheme, it is clear that this represents an oversimplification As is shown in chapter 4, the determination of a value for travel time turns out to be a difficult theoretical and empirical problem, even though people may be seen to trade time for money and money for time. Clearly, ascertaining monetary values for various levels of carbon-monoxide pollution, hydrocarbon pollution, traffic noise, social disruption of neighborhoods and other potential consequences of transportation investment and policies, will be fraught with problems. In the meantime, economic-evaluation techniques cannot take such consequences into account.

The second fault in the economic-evaluation process is the production of a single numeric for each project. This single value tends to obscure the various value judgments and assumptions that must be made in order to undertake an economic evaluation. It also tends to blur distinctions between projects. For example, by employing current value systems, it may not be possible to distinguish between one project that saves 500 people a half hour of travel time every day and one that saves 15,000 people one minute of travel time every day. The decision maker, however, might be sensitive to this distinction, if he were aware of it.

In addition to these inherent flaws, the process of economic evaluation also includes additional faults from the general lack of good input information for the process. First, all but one of the methods requires a discount rate as input, though there is little agreement in the profession on the computation of an appropriate discount rate. Similarly, if correct account is to be taken of the temporal nature of the investment, it is necessary to calculate streams of costs and benefits over the life of the alternatives. This, in turn, requires the ability to forecast the levels of use of a facility, on a year-by-year basis, for the entire life of the alternatives. The ability to make such precise forecasts does not exist at present. It appears that the methods may be quite sensitive to such forecasts, particularly if growth rates may be markedly different for different alternative policies or investments.

Third, the methods depend upon the use of values of both travel-time savings and accidents of varying seriousness. There is little general agreement on what these values should be or even how they should be measured. This is not a trivial concern, since it is shown in chapter 4 that travel-time savings alone constitute a very significant portion of the benefits of many, if not all, construction projects in transportation. Finally, economic evaluation has been restricted to dealing with direct user consequences only. This may be seen to be partly a result of the difficulty of quantifying and monetizing the consequences to nonusers, but has been more specifically a policy decision. It has had the effect, however, of causing the economic-evaluation method to be labeled as seriously incomplete and therefore, wrong.

It may also be noted that the fault of a single numeric value for each alternative is also the greatest advantage of the method. The simplicity of the single value makes the method more clearly used and communicated to nontechnical people. Similarly, the values produced by both the net present worth method and the rate of return method are similar to values used in business. Since many local decision makers are businessmen, unacquainted with the technicalities of transportation-planning methods, these values can be used readily in choosing among alternatives.

Cost-Effectiveness Procedures

In principle, the cost-effectiveness procedure appears to have the capability of overcoming most of the shortcomings of economic-evaluation procedures. Successful use of cost-effectiveness, however, requires both a complete specification of goals and a comprehensive knowledge of the type and extent of the various consequences that may arise from a transportation policy or investment. The procedure has several disadvantages.

First, measures of effectiveness must be developed for all consequences of transportation proposals. As shown in chapter 6, few consequences can be measured in any units, and only broad statements can be made about the directionality of changes in many of the consequences, such as noise, pollution, neighborhood disruption, and property values for various parcels of land. If only directionality is known, it is doubtful whether the procedure will provide a sensitive evaluation mechanism.

Second, the method implies the need for weights for the various consequences. While it is true that such weights will not be hidden in the evaluation process (as may be the case in economic evaluation), there is nevertheless the requirement that the decision maker place weights upon the listed consequences. It appears to be very likely that, when a large number of consequences are enumerated, the judgmental capability of the decision maker may be exceeded. Indeed, one of the principal criticisms of the cost-effectiveness procedure is that it presents too much information, which cannot be readily assimilated and integrated in a decision process.

Finally, the cost-effectiveness process takes no explicit account of the temporal nature of the investment. Costs and consequences (measures of effectiveness) are assessed at a single point in time. Account is not taken of how these may vary over the life of a project. It may be argued that the assessment of consequences is so much in its infancy that it is most improbable that changes in consequences over a ten- to thirty-year period could be determined.

The principal advantages of the cost-effectiveness method are its ability to take account of a full spectrum of consequences on both users and nonusers, and the removal of the need to consider monetization of nonmonetary consequences. In addition, the method renders the evaluation process much more transparent and, at least, invites the decision maker to take a major role in interpreting the evaluation information. In fact, it would probably be correct to say that the method compels the decision maker to become heavily involved through an interpretive and weighting process.

Research Needs

It should be fairly clear that the field of the evaluation of transportation systems, or indeed of any public system, is still relatively poorly developed. There are many issues that have not been resolved satisfactorily and extensive research needs to be done in the identification, measurement, and definition of causality for impacts of transportation investment.

There seems to be little question that the cost-effectiveness procedure is the ideal evaluation scheme, provided that its current shortcomings can be surmounted. Furthermore, it appears to be feasible and potentially valuable to supplement the cost-effectiveness procedure with one of the economic-evaluation procedures, such as the net present value method. In this case, the net present value, as determined from a consideration of those impacts that are monetary or are readily monetized, would be entered either together with, or in place of the direct monetary costs of each alternative. Thus, it does not appear to be appropriate to dismiss all economic-evaluation procedures as making no contribution to an evaluation methodology. On the contrary, it appears to be worthwhile to develop improvements in both procedures simultaneously, towards the goal of a combined evaluation methodology.

A number of specific research tasks can be identified as being necessary to the achievement of such an evaluation methodology. First, it is necessary to achieve considerable improvements in the accuracy and sensitivity of the demand-forecasting process and simultaneous supply estimation. These improvements should obtain far more accurate and sensitive forecasts of travel on any current or planned transportation facility, or of travel under any changed regulatory or control regime. Regardless of whether one is attempting to determine operating-cost changes or travel-time changes within a conventional economic evaluation, or whether one is estimating noise and pollution impacts of a transportation facility, improved capability of forecasting travel is a central requirement.

Second, if continued use is to be made of the economic-evaluation procedures, it is necessary to undertake extensive research into the measurement and use of the value of travel-time savings. A number of issues in this area are raised in chapter 4. Included among these are a resolution of how to measure the value of travel-time savings, to whom they should be applied, whether it is appropriate to use personal time values in a public-viewpoint evaluation, and how to forecast values of travel-time savings over the life of a transportation project. These and a number of other issues were set out in detail by a recent conference[4] that was concerned with defining research needs and directions in value of time as well as behavioral travel demand.

Within the cost-effectiveness approach, the primary research need is to develop improved impact information. There are a number of elements to such research. First, it is necessary to develop improved information on what impacts are caused by various types of transportation investment. Following this, a great deal of research effort is needed to determine the extent of the various impacts that may occur and to develop an understanding of how these impacts arise. In particular, such research should be designed to determine how favorable impacts can be maximized and unfavorable ones ameliorated. Thus, impact analysis should be designed to go beyond a mere accounting of the impacts and move towards a prescriptive science. A further element of impact research is the development of procedures to weight impacts within a cost-effectiveness framework, so that the decision maker is not swamped with information. This may require the development of a common metric of impacts, such as is envisaged in the energy-flow approach, or it may require an extensive educational effort designed to assist the decision maker to handle the vast amounts of information produced by the cost-effectiveness approach. Finally, impact research is required to determine the effect of time on each type of impact. Before the cost-effectiveness approach can be considered to be fully operational, it must be able to produce estimates of the impacts over the life of each alternative being considered.

The last major area requiring research is that of the incorporation of uncertainty into the evaluation process. Since transportation alternatives generally have lives measured in years, there must always be considerable uncertainty in the period of the life of each alternative strategy. This uncertainty must be incorporated in the evaluation in such a way that the decision maker can understand the effects of uncertainty on each alternative and evaluate the alternatives accordingly. Recent research[5] has attempted to develop such capabilities through the use of Bayesian statistics[6] and related concepts. Much additional progress is still needed in this work before operational procedures are achieved that take account of uncertainty over the project life.

Notes

Notes

Chapter 1
Purpose and Basic Concepts of Evaluation

1. Martin Wohl and Brian V. Martin, *Traffic Systems Analysis for Engineers and Planners*, New York: McGraw-Hill Book Co., 1967, pp. 181-183; Eugene L. Grant and W. Grant Ireson, *Principles of Engineering Economy*, New York: The Ronald Press Co., Fifth Edition, 1970, pp. 10, 136-137.

2. See for example, Grant and Ireson, *Engineering Economy*, pp. 456-457; Tillo E. Kuhn, *Public Enterprise Economics and Transport Problems*, Berkeley, California: University of California Press, 1962, p. 13; R. Zettel, "Highway Benefit and Cost Analysis as an Aid to Investment Decisions," Institute of Transportation and Traffic Engineering, reprint number 49, University of California, Berkeley, California, 1956.

3. Grant and Ireson, *Engineering Economy*, p. 136.

4. Peter R. Stopher and Arnim H. Meyburg, *Urban Transportation Modeling and Planning*, Lexington, Massachusetts: Lexington Books, D.C.Heath and Co., 1975, pp. 15-24.

5. Wohl and Martin, *Traffic Systems Analysis*, pp. 183-185; Grant and Ireson, *Engineering Economy*, pp. 136-137.

6. Edwin N. Thomas and Joseph L. Schofer, "Strategies for the Evaluation of Alternative Transportation Plans," *NCHRP Project Report No. 96*, Washington, D.C.: Highway Research Board, 1970.

7. Radnor J. Paquette, Norman Ashford, and Paul H. Wright, *Transportation Engineering Planning and Design*, New York: The Ronald Press Co., 1972, p. 236.

Chapter 2
Costs, Prices, Benefits, and Consumer Surplus

1. Wohl and Martin, *Traffic Systems Analysis*, p. 186; Paquette, Ashford and Wright, *Transportation Engineering*, p. 236; Robley Winfrey, *Economic Analysis for Transportation—A Guide for Decision Makers*, Washington, D.C.: Highway Users Federation for Safety and Mobility, 1971, p. 4.

2. See chapter 6, pp. 113-115.

3. M.H. West, "Economic Value of Time Savings in Traffic," *Proceedings of the Institute of Traffic Engineers*, 1946, number XVII.

4. The current state of the art of measurement of comfort and convenience is described in several documents. See, for example, Stopher and Meyburg, *Urban Transportation Modeling*, pp. 312-313; Gregory C. Nicolaidis, "Quantification of the Comfort Variable," *Transportation Research*, 1975, volume 9, number 1, pp. 55-66; Bruce D. Spear, "The Development of a Generalized Convenience Variable for Models of Mode Choice," unpublished Ph.D. dissertation, Cornell University, Department of Environmental Engineering, Ithaca, New York, June 1974.

5. A more detailed discussion is given in chapter 6, p. 99.

6. Grant and Ireson, *Engineering Economy*, pp. 136-137.

7. Stopher and Meyburg, *Urban Transportation Modeling*, chapter 3.

8. Wohl and Martin, *Traffic Systems Analysis*, p. 192.

9. Ibid., pp. 191-196; Robley Winfrey, "Consumer Surplus does not Apply to Highway Transportation Economy," *Transportation Research Record Number 550*, 1975, pp. 1-19.

10. This view has been espoused by several others, for example, Herbert Mohring and M. Harwitz, *Highway Benefits - An Analytical Framework*, Evanston, Illinois: Northwestern University Press, 1962; Kuhn, *Public Enterprise Economics*, chapter IV; D.J.Reynolds, "The Assessment of Priority for Road Improvements," Road Research Technical Paper Number 48, Road Research Laboratory, Crowthorne, Berks, England, 1960; Christopher D. Foster and Michael E. Beesley, "Estimating the Social Benefit of Constructing an Underground Railway in London," *Journal of the Royal Statistical Society*, 1963, volume 126, part 1, p. 48.

11. Stopher and Meyburg, *Urban Transportation Modeling*, pp. 47-48; Wohl and Martin, *Traffic Systems Analysis*, p. 197.

12. Wohl and Martin, *Traffic Systems Analysis*, pp. 208-210.

Chapter 3
Economic Principles of Interest and Capital Recovery

1. Grant and Ireson, *Engineering Economy*, p. 25.

2. Wohl and Martin, *Traffic Systems Analysis*, pp. 217-222.

3. Grant and Ireson, *Engineering Economy*, pp. 34-35.

4. Ibid., pp. 26-32, 34-37.

5. Ibid., p. 36; Wohl and Martin, *Traffic Systems Analysis*, p. 215.

6. Wohl and Martin, *Traffic Systems Analysis*, pp. 222-226.

7. H. Raiffa, *Decision Analysis*, Reading, Massachusetts: Addison-

Wesley Publishing Co., 1968; R. Schaifler, *Probability and Statistics for Business Decisions*, New York: McGraw-Hill Book Co., 1959.

8. D.V. Lindley, "Bayesian Statistics, A Review," *Society for Industrial and Applied Mathematics*, Philadelphia, Pennsylvania, 1971.

Chapter 4
The Value of Time Savings

1. West, "Economic Value of Time Savings."

2. As is seen later in this chapter, one possible position is to derive the value of travel time as a whole and apply this value to any time savings. This is done in classical economic theory. This procedure then dictates that variation in values of time savings depend upon trip purpose only. While being a useful theoretical derivation, this approach does not seem to be behaviorally consistent.

3. David A. Hensher, "The Consumer's Choice Function: A Study of Traveller Behaviour and Values," unpublished Ph.D. dissertation, School of Economics, University of New South Wales, Kensington, NSW, Australia, October 1972, p. 74.

4. G.H. Fallon, et al., "Benefits of Interstate Highways," *Committee Print (91-41), U.S. Government Printing Office*, Washington, D.C., 1970.

5. T.M. Coburn, M.E. Beesley, and D.J. Reynolds, "The London-Birmingham Motorway Traffic and Economics," *Road Research Technical Paper Number 46*, Her Majesty's Stationery Office, 1960; D. Barrell, "Cost-Benefit Analysis in Transportation Planning," Oxford University, England, Oxford Working Papers in Planning Education and Research, Oxford University, England, April 1972, pp. 37 and 40.

6. Foster and Beesley, "Estimating the Social Benefit"; Barrell, "Cost-Benefit Analysis," pp. 42-43.

7. N.R. Gillhespy, "The Tay Road Bridge—A Case Study," *Scottish Journal of Political Economy*, June 1968; Barrell, "Cost-Benefit Analysis," pp. 48-49.

8. It should be noted that this definition has not always been applied rigorously in the past. For example, in the valuation of intercity air travel for business, both Gronau and DeVany used all air travelers on business, or even all air travelers. Since much of the travel for intercity business trips occurs outside normal business hours, it is not clear that this can be considered to be working time travel.

9. Reuben Gronau, "The Effect of Traveling Time on the Demand

for Passenger Transportation,'' *Journal of Political Economy*, 1970, volume 78, number 2.

10. A. DeVany, *The Value of Time in Air Travel: Theory and Evidence*, Research Contribution 162, Center for Naval Analyses, University of Rochester, Rochester, New York, April 1971.

11. Shalom Reichman, ''Subjective Time Savings in Inter-Urban Travel, An Empirical Study,'' unpublished mimeo, Hebrew University of Jerusalem, Jerusalem, 1973.

12. R.J. Fullerton and D. Cooper, ''A Pilot Study on the Effect of Road Improvements on the Marginal Wage Increment,'' Report to the U.K. Ministry of Transport from Associated Industrial Consultants (AIC) Ltd., May 1969; Makrotest Ltd., ''Study into the Assessment of the Marginal Wage Increment - Short Term Savings,'' Report to the U.K. Ministry of Transport, London, June 1970; N. Rubashaw, R. Michali, C. Taylor and R. Key, ''A Study of the Long Term Marginal Wage Increment,'' *Time Research Note Number 23*, London: Highway Economics Unit, Department of the Environment, May, 1971; David A. Hensher, ''Review of Studies Leading to Existing Values of Travel Time,'' *Transportation Research Board Special Report* (forthcoming), Washington, D.C.: Transportation Research Board, National Academy of Sciences.

13. Hensher, ''Review of Studies.''

14. U.S. Bureau of Public Roads and the Cook County Highway Department, ''A Study of Highway Traffic and the Highway System of Cook County, Illinois,'' unpublished report, 1925.

15. W.R. Bellis, ''Highway Traffic Analysis, Planning and Economics,'' New Jersey Highway Department Lecture Series, Paper 6, 1947; D.W. Glassborow, ''The Road Research Laboratory's Investment Criterion Examined,'' *Bulletin of Oxford University Institute of Statistics*, 1960, volume 22, number 4.

16. Daniel G. Haney, ''The Value of Time for Passenger Cars: A Theoretical Analysis and Description of Preliminary Experiments,'' Final Report, volume 1, Menlo Park, California: Stanford Research Institute, May 1967.

17. Francois X. de Donnea, *The Determinants of Transport Mode Choice in Dutch Cities: Some Disaggregate, Stochastic Models*, Rotterdam, The Netherlands: Rotterdam University Press, 1971; Hensher, ''The Consumer's Choice Function''; Peter L. Watson, *The Value of Time, Behaviorial Models of Mode Choice*, Lexington, Massachusetts: Lexington Books, D.C. Heath and Co., 1974.

18. de Donnea, *The Determinants of Mode Choice*.

19. Ibid., p. 27.

20. Hensher, "The Consumer's Choice Function"; Watson, *The Value of Time*.

21. Watson, *The Value of Time*, pp. 51-53.

22. Peter R. Stopher, "The Derivation of Values of Time," *Transportation Research Board Special Report*, (forthcoming); Kenneth C. Rogers, "Derivation of Values of Time from Behavioral Models," position paper for Second International Conference on Behavioral Travel Demand, Asheville, North Carolina, May 1975.

23. Kenneth C. Rogers, Gillian M. Townsend, and Alex E. Metcalf, *Planning for the Work Journey*, Reading, England: Local Government Operational Research Unit, Report Number C67, April 1970.

24. Peter L. Watson and Peter R. Stopher, "The Effect of Income on the Usage and Valuation of Transport Modes," *Transportation Research Forum Proceedings*, 1974, volume XV, number 1, pp. 460-469.

25. Hensher, "The Consumer's Choice Function."

26. Ibid., pp. 85-86.

27. It should be noted that the authors feel that only stratification is a valid behavioral construct for such an investigation, particularly given the statistical problems of interactive variables. This position is argued more lengthily in Stopher and Meyburg, *Urban Transportation Modeling*.

28. Michael E. Beesley, "The Value of Time Spent in Travelling: Some New Evidence," *Economica*, 1965, volume XXXII, number 126.

29. If the axes are plotted the other way around, i.e., with the time difference on the horizontal axis and the cost difference on the vertical axis, the misclassifications will be above the line.

30. Michael E. Beesley and Peter R. Stopher, "Time Values and Modal-Split Estimation," unpublished paper, March 1975.

31. Hensher, "Review of Studies"; Anthony J. Harrison and David A. Quarmby, "The Value of Time in Transport Planning - A Review," Mathematical Advisory Unit Note 154, London: Department of the Environment, December 1969.

32. U.S. Bureau of Public Roads, "Study of Highway Traffic."

33. C.M. Hummel, "A Criterion Designed to Aid Highway Expenditure Programming," *Highway Research Board Bulletin Number 249*, Washington, D.C., 1960.

34. Lavis calculated a value of 60¢ per vehicle-hour from considering operating costs (see F. Lavis, "Highways as Elements of Transportation," *Transactions of the American Society of Civil Engineers*, 1931, volume 95), and Morrison calculated a value of $1.20 per vehicle-hour from three studies of toll-free choices (R.L. Morrison, "Side Lights on Highway Economics," *Civil Engineering*, August 1931).

35. Daniel G. Haney, *The Value of Time for Passenger Cars: A Theoretical Analysis and Description of Preliminary Experiments*, Final Report, volume I, Menlo Park, California: Stanford Research Institute, May 1967; Thomas C. Thomas, *The Value of Time for Passenger Cars; An Experimental Study of Commuters' Values*, Final Report, Volume II, Menlo Park, California: Stanford Research Institute, May 1967.

36. Thomas C. Thomas and Gordon I. Thompson, *The Value of Time Saved by Trip Purpose*, Report to Bureau of Public Roads, USDOT, Menlo Park, California: Stanford Research Institute, October 1970.

37. Stopher and Meyburg, *Urban Transportation Modeling*, chapter 16.

38. Thomas, *The Value of Time for Passenger Cars*.

39. Thomas C. Thomas and Gordon I. Thompson, "The Value of Time for Commuting Motorists as a Function of Their Income Level and Amount of Time Saved," *Highway Research Record Number 314*, 1970, p. 13.

40. Thomas and Thompson, *The Value of Time*; Thomas and Thompson, "The Value of Time for Commuting Motorists," pp. 1-19; Thomas C. Thomas and Gordon I. Thompson, "Value of Time Saved by Trip Purpose." *Highway Research Record Number 369*, 1971, pp. 104-117.

41. Thomas and Thompson, *The Value of Time*; Thomas and Thompson, "The Value of Time for Commuting Motorists," (with discussion by Thomas E. Lisco and Peter R. Stopher); Thomas and Thompson, "Value of Time Saved," (with discussion by Shalom Reichman).

42. Thomas and Thompson, *The Value of Time*, pp. 7-16.

43. See for example Stopher and Meyburg, *Urban Transportation Modeling*, pp. 290-292.

44. Watson and Stopher and Stopher and Meyburg have argued that the interactive term is not behaviorally sound or computationally appropriate. (Watson and Stopher, "The Effect of Income"; and Stopher and Meyburg, *Urban Transportation Modeling*, pp. 310-311.)

45. Hensher, "The Consumer's Choice Function"; and Hensher, "Review of Studies."

46 P. Merlin and M. Barbier, *Study of the Modal Split Between Car and Public Transport*, Paris: Institut d'Amenagement et d'Urbanisme de la Region Parisienne, 1965.

47. Beesley, "The Value of Time Spent Travelling."

48. David A. Quarmby, "Choice of Travel Mode for the Journey to Work: Some Findings," *Journal of Transport Economics and Policy*, 1967, volume 1, number 3.

49. Charles A. Lave, "The Demand for Urban Mass Transportation,"

Review of Economics and Statistics, 1970, volume 52, number 3, pp. 320-323.

50. Thomas E. Lisco, "The Value of Commuters' Travel Time: A Study in Urban Transportation," unpublished Ph.D. dissertation, Department of Economics, University of Chicago, Chicago, 1967.

51. Hensher, "The Consumer's Choice Function."

52. Gökmen Ergün, "Development of a Downtown Parking Model," *Highway Research Record Number 369*, 1971, pp. 118-134.

53. Hensher, "Review of Studies."

54. Watson, *The Value of Time*.

55. Hensher, "The Consumer's Choice Function."

56. Beesley, "The Value of Time Spent Travelling."

57. Ergün, "Development of a Downtown Parking Model."

58. Beesley and Stopher, "Time Values and Modal-Split Estimation."

Chapter 5
Methods of Evaluation

1. Wohl and Martin, *Traffic Systems Analysis*.

2. Ibid.

3. Ian G. Heggie, *Transport Engineering Economics*, London: McGraw-Hill Book Co., 1972; Nancy W. Sheldon and Robert Brandwein, *The Economics and Social Impact of Investments in Public Transit*, Lexington, Massachusetts: Lexington Books, D.C. Heath and Co., 1973.

4. Wohl and Martin, *Traffic Systems Analysis*, pp. 252, et seq.

5. Wohl and Martin, *Traffic Systems Analysis*.

6. Grant and Ireson, *Engineering Economy*; Wohl and Martin, *Traffic Systems Analysis*; Gerald A. Fleischer, "Numerator-Denominator Issue in the Calculation of Benefit-Cost Ratios," *Highway Research Record Number 383*, Washington D.C., 1972, pp. 27-30.

7. E.L. Grant, "Interest and the Rate of Return on Investments," *Highway Research Board Special Report 56*, Washington, D.C., 1960; Grant and Ireson, *Engineering Economy*; Martin Wohl, "Clarifying the Ambiguities of Internal Rate of Return Method Versus Net Present Value Method for Analyzing Mutually Exclusive Alternatives," *Transportation Research Record 550*, 1975, pp. 48-59.

8. Wohl and Martin, *Traffic Systems Analysis*, p. 230.

9. Ibid.

10. Ibid., p. 237.

Chapter 6
The Identification, Measurement and Interpretation of Impact

1. Phillip B. Goodwin, "On the Evaluation of Human Life in Accident Studies," *Accident, Analysis and Prevention*, volume 5, 1973, pp. 287-293; Barbara Sabey, "Accidents: Their Cost and Relation to Surface Characteristics," paper presented to Symposium on Safety and the Concrete Road Surface—Design, Specification and Construction, Birmingham, England, November 1973.

2. Goodwin, "Evaluation of Human Life," p. 287.

3. Michael J. Demetsky and Frank D. Shepard, "Measuring the Impact of a New Urban Highway on Community Traffic," *Traffic Engineering*, 1972 (July), pp. 42-45; and Lester A. Hoel "Latent Demand for Urban Transportation," Transportation Research, Inc., Carnegie-Mellon University, Pittsburgh, Pennsylvania, 1968.

4. Harlan W. Gilmore, *Transportation and the Growth of Cities*, Glencoe, Illinois, The Free Press, 1963.

5. Charles E. Lee, *Sixty Years of the Northern*, London Transport, London, England, 1967.

6. U.S. Department of Transportation, Federal Highway Administration, "Policy and Procedure Memorandum 20-8," Washington, D.C., January 14, 1969.

7. Marvin L. Manheim, et al., "Transportation Decision-Making—A Guide to Social and Environmental Consideration," *NCHRP Report 156*, Transportation Research Board, Washington, D.C., 1975.

8. For example, the Cabrini-Green development in Chicago, resulting partly from the construction of the Dan Ryan Expressway.

9. Floyd Thiel, "Social Effects of Modern Highway Transportation," *Public Roads*, April 1962, pp. 1-10.

10. Edwin N. Thomas and Joseph L. Schofer, "Information Requirements for Evaluating the Social Impacts of Transportation Investments," from *Transportation: A Service*, New York: N.Y. Academy of Sciences, 1967, pp. 101-116.

11. Ibid., p. 106.

12. Raymond H. Ellis, "Some Comments on Social Impacts and Urban Transportation Planning," *ASME Transportation Engineering Conference*, 1968, pp. 276-285.

13. Jon E. Burkhardt, "The Impact of Highways on Urban Neighborhoods: A Model of Social Change," *Highway Research Record 356*, Washington, D.C.: pp. 85-97, 1971.

14. S.L. Hill and B. Frankland, "Mobility as a Measure of Neighborhood," *Highway Research Record No. 187*, 1967, pp. 33-42.

15. R.G. McGinnis, "Relocation Impact Index," unpublished MS Thesis, Northwestern University, Evanston, Illinois, 1969.

16. S.L. Hill and B. Frankland, "Mobility as a Measure of Neighborhood."

17. R.G. McGinnis, "Relocation Impact Index."

18. James D. Chalupnik (ed.), *Transportation Noises*, University of Washington Press, Seattle, Washington, 1970; OECD, *Urban Traffic Noise—Strategy for an Improved Environment*, Paris, France, 1971; U.S. Department of Transportation, Office of the Secretary, "Transportation Noise and its Control," DOT P5630.1, June 1972; Erich K. Bender, "On the Generation and Reduction of Automotive and Rail-Vehicle Noise," *Proceedings 16th Annual Technical Meeting*, Institute of Environmental Sciences, Boston, Massachusetts, 1970, pp. 221-227.

19. M.C.P. Underwood, "A Preliminary Investigation into Lorry Tyre Noise," Transport and Road Research Laboratory, Department of the Environment, TRRL Report LR 601, 1973; D.G. Harland, "Rolling Noise and Vehicle Noise," Crowthorne Berks, England: Transport and Road Research Laboratory, Department of the Environment, TRRL Report LR 652, 1974.

20. W.H.T. Holden, "Sound Levels and Rapid Transit," *City and Suburban Travel*, April 1961, issue 3E.

21. This was observed by one of the authors while working in such a location.

22. H.C. McKee and K.D. Mills, "A Comparison of Various Sources of Automotive Emissions," *Journal of Air Pollution Control Association*, 1961, volume 2, pp. 516-522.

23. Ibid.

24. Ibid.

25. J.A. Maga and J.R. Kinosian, "Motor Vehicle Emission Standards—Present and Future," Society of Automotive Engineers, N.Y., *N.Y. Paper No. 660104*, 1966.

26. "Report on Bi-State Study of the Air Pollution in the Chicago Metropolitan Area," Illinois Department of Public Health, Indiana State Board of Health and Purdue University, 1957-59.

27. R. Scorer, *Air Pollution*, Elmsford, New York: Pergamon Press, 1968.

28. P.H. Parkin, H.J. Purkis, R.J. Stephenson and B. Schlaffenberg, "London Noise Survey," London: Her Majesty's Stationery Office, 1968.

29. J.L. Beaton and L. Bourget, "Can Noise Radiation from Highways Be Reduced by Design?" paper presented at 47th Annual Highway Research Board Meeting, Washington, D.C.: 1968.

30. Colin G. Gordon, et al., "Highway Noise—A Design Guide for Highway Engineers," *NCHRP Report 117*, Highway Research Board, Washington, D.C., 1971; M.D. Harmelink and J.J. Hajek, "Noise Barrier Evaluation and Alternatives for Highway Noise Control," Ontario Ministry of Transportation and Communications, MTC Report No. RR 180, Toronto: September 1972.

31. Howard T. Odum, *Environment, Power, and Society*, New York: Wiley-Interscience, 1971.

32. Mitchell J. Lavine and Arnim H. Meyburg, "Toward Environmental Benefit/Cost Analysis—Measurement Methodology," Final Report, *NCHRP Project 20-11A*, May 1976; ongoing joint research project between Florida Department of Transportation and the University of Florida, Gainesville, Department of Environmental Engineering Sciences (Suzanne Bayley and William E. Kirksey, principal investigators); "The Value of Highways to a Region Including the Impact of Highway Construction on the Value of Natural Areas," ongoing research project at the University of Florida, Gainesville, sponsored by the U.S. Army Corps of Engineers (Suzanne Bayley and James Zuichetto, principal investigators), "Energetics Analysis of Alternative Bulk Commodity Inland Transportation Systems."

Chapter 7
Cost-Effectiveness

1. Richard deNeufville and Joseph A. Stafford, *Systems Analysis for Engineers and Managers*, New York: McGraw-Hill Book Co., 1971; J. Morley English (ed.), *Cost-Effectiveness—The Economic Evaluation of Engineered Systems*, New York: John Wiley and Sons, 1968; Edward N. Dodson, "Cost-Effectiveness in Urban Transportation," *Operations Research*,1969, volume 17, number 3, pp. 373-394; Michael B. Teitz, "Cost Effectiveness: A Systems Approach to Analysis of Urban Services," *American Institute of Planners Journal*, September 1968, pp. 303-311.

2. deNeufville and Stafford, *Systems Analysis for Engineers and Managers*.

3. Based on Thomas and Schofer, "Strategies for the Evaluation of Alternative Transportation Plans."

4. Peter R. Stopher, "On the Application of Psychological Measurement Techniques to the Estimation of Travel Demand," *Environment and Behavior*, (forthcoming); Richard M. Michaels, "Public Policy Development: The Matrix for Decision Making," paper presented to 55th Annual Meeting of the Transportation Research Board, Washington, D.C.: January 1976; and George L. Peterson, Robert S. Gemmell, and Joseph L. Schofer, "Assessment of Environmental Impacts: Multidisciplinary Judgments of Large-Scale Projects," *Ekistics*, 1974, number 218, pp. 23-30.

5. Charles J. Hitch and Roland N. McKean, *The Economics of Defense in the Nuclear Age*, New York: Atheneum, 1970; Peter D. Fox, "A Theory of Cost-Effectiveness for Military Systems Analysis," *Operations Research*, 1965, volume 13, number 2, pp. 191-201.

6. Samuel A. Schmitt, *Measuring Uncertainty: An Elementary Introduction to Bayesian Statistics*, Reading, Massachusetts: Addison-Wesley Publishing Company, 1969.

7. E.S. Quade, "Cost-Effectiveness: An Introduction and Overview," *Transportation Journal*, Summer 1966, pp. 5-13.

8. Hitch and McKean, *The Economics of Defense in the Nuclear Age*.

9. Herman Zabronsky, "A Mathematical Theory of Cost-Effectiveness," 1967, *Socio-Economic Planning Science*, volume 1, pp. 3-18; Edward N. Dodson, "Demand Functions, Behavioral Analysis, and Cost Effectiveness in Urban Transportation," *Transportation Science*, 1975, volume 9, number 2, pp. 139-148.

10. Edwin N. Thomas, and Joseph L. Schofer, "Strategies for the Evaluation of Alternative Transportation Plans," *NCHRP Project Report No. 96*, Highway Research Board, Washington, D.C.: 1970, p. 58.

11. Ibid., pp. 60-61.

12. Thomas and Schofer, "Strategies for the Evaluation of Alternative Transportation Plans."

13. Ibid., p. 64.

14. Thilo Sarrazin, Frithjof Spreer, and Manfred Tietzel, "Logical Decision-Making Techniques to Evaluate Public Investment Projects: Cost-Benefit Analysis, Cost-Effectiveness Analysis, Utility Analysis—A Critical Comparative Approach," *International Journal of Transportation Economics*, August 1974, pp. 155-170.

15. U.S. Department of Transportation, "Policy and Procedure Memorandum 20-8."

16. Ibid.

Chapter 8
Summary and Conclusions

1. U.S. Department of Transportation, "Policy and Procedure Memorandum 20-8."

2. David Callies, "Value Capture Policy: Its Potentials and Achievability," paper presented to 55th Annual Meeting of the Transportation Research Board, Washington, D.C.: January 1976.

3. *Van Nostrand's Scientific Encyclopedia*, Princeton, New Jersey: Van Nostrand Co., 1968, p. 1185.

4. Peter R. Stopher and Arnim H. Meyburg, *Behavioral Travel-Demand Models*, Lexington, Massachusetts: Lexington Books, D.C. Heath and Co., (forthcoming, 1976.)

5. Lonnie E. Haefner and Edward K. Morlok, "Optimal Geometric Design Decisions for Highway Safety," *Highway Research Record Number 371*, 1971, pp. 12-23; Lonnie E. Haefner, "Optimal Statistical Decisions in Highway Safety Related to Geometric Design," unpublished Ph.D. dissertation, Department of Civil Engineering, Northwestern University, Evanston, Illinois, August 1970.

6. Schmitt, *Measuring Uncertainty*.

Index

Index

abandonment, 71, 86

accessibility, 15, 100, 109, 110, 112, 115, 116, 121, 122, 123, 136, 137, 152

accidents, 98, 99, 151, 152, 153. *See also* costs

action plans, 103

activity linkages, 117, 118, 119, 121, 122; opportunities, 116; sets, 116, 117, 118, 119, 120, 123

air polution, 15, 123, 126-128, 129, 130, 136, 137, 155, 156

alternative: dominant, 48; inferior, 48

annexation, 113

annual average daily traffic, 72

annual-costs method, 68-84, 86, 89, 93

annual traffic volume, 69, 72, 74

assets, 34

average annual volume, 84

average daily traffic, 68, 70

Bayesian statistics, 35, 141, 157

Beesley, M.E., 39, 51, 63, 66

benefit cost ratio, 67, 86-89, 135, 151

benefits, 5, 7, 11, 14-15, 24-27, 67, 70, 71, 75, 82, 84, 86, 94, 111; annual, 76, 88; direct, 37, 119; discounted annual, 76, 80; discounted project, 91; highway, 98; highway engineer's definition, 20; measurement, 16; net, 15; nonmonetary, 93, 151; nonperceived user, 67; nonuser, 15, 67; perceived, 15, 16-21, 67; social, 15; total annual, 75, 77, 79; unperceived, 15; user travel, 15, 39, 70, 79

Bureau of Public Roads, 59, 60

capacity, 22; capital recovery, 29-35; factor, 32, 68, 82; output volume, 22

carbon monoxide, 126, 127, 154

cause and effect relationship, 7

Civil Rights Act of 1964, 103; of 1968, 103

Clean Air Act, 1970, 103

comfort, 14, 45, 47, 64

competitive economy, 34

congestion, 15

consequences, 5, 98, 99, 100, 104, 109, 116, 117, 118, 119, 122, 139, 141, 142, 143, 146, 151, 155, 156

consumer surplus, 11, 16-21, 53, 151

convenience, 14, 58, 65; difference, 58

cost difference, 58

cost-effectiveness, 135-149, 151, 152, 153, 156, 157

cost models, 140, 145

cost preferrer, 52, 54

costs, 5, 7, 11, 58, 67, 70, 84, 86, 88, 89, 92, 94, 139-141, 156; accident, 11, 14, 99, 153; administration, 11, 12, 14; annual, 67, 68, 93; average annual user, 68; capital, 67, 68, 70, 79, 140, 151; construction, 11, 12, 67, 79, 140; continuing, 68, 79; direct operating, 12; discounted project, 91; financing, 140; garaging, 14, 21; gasoline, 21; highway investment, 13; indirect operating, 12; land acquisition, 11, 12; maintenance, 11, 12, 67, 68, 70, 73, 81, 140, 151; management, 140; marginal, 13, 140; marginal operating, 13; mobile components, 140; monetary, 93; net, 15; nonmonetary, 93, 151; nonstatutory, 12; operation, 11, 12, 67, 68, 73, 81, 140, 151; out-of-pocket, 21; parking, 14; present value of user, 69; research and development, 140; right-of-way acquisition, 140; shipping, 15; short-run, 21; social, 12; statutory relocation, 11, 12; terminal, 12, 14, 67, 99, 140; time, 13, 21, 67, 71, 73, 153; toll, 21; traveled-way structural, 140; user travel, 11, 12, 70, 73, 76, 98, 99; vehicle ownership, 12, 13, 14, 21,

175

About the Authors

Peter R. Stopher is associate professor of civil engineering and Director of Research of the Transportation Center at Northwestern University. He was born in Crowborough, England, and was educated at University College London, where he received the B.Sc. in civil and municipal engineering in 1964 and the Ph.D. in traffic studies in 1967. From 1967 to 1968, he was a research officer with the Greater London Council. Subsequently, he has held faculty appointments at Cornell University, McMaster University (Ontario), and Northwestern University, specializing in urban transportation.

Dr. Stopher has been a consultant to a number of private firms and to governmental agencies on various aspects of urban transportation planning, travel demand, and impacts of transportation facilities. He is the joint author with Dr. Arnim H. Meyburg of *Urban Transportation Modeling and Planning*. He has also written a number of technical papers, principally in travel-demand modeling and travel-time valuation, as well as in urban goods movement, and in statistical and psychological methods. He is a member of several professional societies and committees in both the United States and the United Kingdom.

Arnim H. Meyburg is associate professor of transportation planning and engineering in the School of Civil and Environmental Engineering at Cornell University. Born in Bremerhaven, West Germany, he was educated at the University of Hamburg, Germany, the Free University of Berlin, Germany, and at Northwestern University, Evanston, Illinois. He received a M.S. in quantitative geography in 1968 and a Ph.D. in civil engineering (transportation) in 1971, both from Northwestern University. From 1968 to 1969, he was a research associate at the Transportation Center of Northwestern University. Dr. Meyburg has been a faculty member at Cornell University since 1969. He held a visiting appointment at the University of California at Irvine during the fall of 1975 and at the Technical University of Munich during the summer of 1976.

Dr. Meyburg has also been a consultant to private industry and several governmental agencies. In addition to being joint author with Dr. Stopher of an earlier book, he has written a number of technical papers in the subject areas of travel-demand modeling, urban goods movement, and transportation-systems analysis. He is a member of several professional societies and committees.